"There is much here to help you ___ church life, even if you see it ___ ___ ___. Unmuddle your ecclesiastical gray matter by reading and contemplating these challenging principles."

Jim Elliff, **Baptist Pastor, Missouri**

"A compelling and thorough Biblical case for the modern church returning to some of the foundational practices of the early church with very practical steps to help the pastor institute these practices in today's church. With over 40 years of pastoral experience, I can truthfully say this book should be required reading for all church planters."

A.T. Stewart, **Baptist Pastor, Georgia**

"An ecclesiology rooted in New Testament church practice rather than in the shifting sands of contemporary church growth fads. After establishing normative church practice from NT church patterns, the author then gives pragmatic ways those practices can be implemented within modern western culture, thus happily integrating practice with theology. This book is a godsend for those frustrated by the failures of modern evangelical 'models' for church practice, and for those who are discovering that the model provided by the Holy Spirit-inspired apostles is the most practical model of them all."

Dan Trotter, **Missionary**

"In a day where 'How To' is rarely backed up with 'Why To', a work arrives where these thoughts meet. This timely resource is supported by timeless Biblical insights to assist those who seek to put into practice what many simply theorize about. Convincing, convicting, and illuminating, this handbook provides a glimpse into how church life was in the first century and how it can be in this century.

Tim Andrews, **Church Planter, Pastor, Georgia**

"A great practical tool for pastors, church planters, missionaries, and all Christians seeking to live out basic cross-cultural New Testament Church principles in local churches today."

Joshua B., **Baptist Missionary**

"When sound exegesis and practical application meet together you get a book like Steve's where he not only discusses the theological principals of New Testament Church dynamics but also discusses how to put them into practice in the context of the local assembly. Participatory worship, the Lord's Supper as a full meal, small church model, and much more—he leaves no stone unturned. This book is a must read for anyone interested in New Testament Church practices and how to transition or implement them in your own context whether it be house church, traditional church, or anything in between."

Paul A. Kaiser, **Baptist Pastor, California**

"The Lord began to reveal to me what his church should be like. The information in this book became my foundation. It very accurately and thoroughly details all the legacies left to us by the apostles of Jesus Christ. They left a pattern for us to build a church, such as it should be. The individual pieces of my understanding of the church this material folded into the whole picture."

Andrey Milkin, **Church Planter, Russia**

"The antidote to the evangelical obsession with the 'bigger is better' model of church organisation. It is not a cure-all panacea for the many ills in the church today; however it is the start of a conversation that may—with God's help—lead to much-needed reform. If you would like to know what church patterned after New Testament principles and practices looks like, then New Testament Church Dynamics is for you."

Robert Millar, **Baptist Pastor, N. Ireland**

NEW TESTAMENT CHURCH DYNAMICS

Help for Bi-Vocational, House Church, and Small-Church Pastors Drawn from Early Church Practice

2nd Edition

Stephen E. Atkerson

Special Thanks to Lixin Atkerson for layout and artwork.

New Testament Church Dynamics, Second Edition

Stephen E. Atkerson

© 2017, 2024 by New Testament Reformation Fellowship (NTRF.org)
Atlanta, Georgia

ISBN 978-0-9729082-6-9

Table of Contents

Introduction

Every New Testament church letter was written to an illegal congregation that met secretly in someone's home, often under bi-vocational leadership. The ecclesiology presented in the epistles was thus *designed* for effectively shepherding smaller churches. The result? God's kingdom spread like yeast throughout the Roman Empire.

I've served as a bi-vocational small-church leader for over thirty years, and am well aware of its challenges. Over that time, the effectiveness of my ministry has been greatly increased by shepherding in the context of early church practice. The church has thrived both spiritually and relationally in amazing ways. Today's small church leaders can have a big disciple-making impact in the context of first-century ecclesiology.

Jesus said: "No one pours new wine into old wineskins. If he does, the wine will burst the skins, and both the wine and the wineskins will be ruined. No, he pours new wine into new wineskins."[1] His point was simply that some actions are inappropriate. Borrowing Jesus' illustration, if we were to compare the new wine to pastoral ministry, then the wineskins might be likened to ecclesiology.

---

[1] Mark 2:22. After waiting patiently for Job's three friends to finish speaking, Elihu said, "Behold, my belly is like wine that has no vent; like new wineskins ready to burst. I must speak, that I may find relief ..." (Job 32:19-20).

Arguably, the best wineskin for shepherding is found in the dynamic small-church practices of the New Testament. *Who knew better than Jesus the best church-practice wineskins for training people to obey all that He commanded?*

Dynamic New Testament small-church ecclesiology was *simple*—a family atmosphere, "each one has" participatory meetings, a focus on one-another ministry, weekly fellowship over food, genuine servant leadership, and the in-depth discussion of Scripture. Economist E.F. Schumacher said, "Any intelligent fool can make things bigger and more complex. It takes a lot of genius and a lot of courage to move in the opposite direction."[2] First century small-church practices create the ideal context for church leaders to uplift Jesus, "warning everyone and teaching everyone with all wisdom, that we may present everyone mature in Christ."[3]

The milieu for dynamic disciple making in those early small churches was also *strategic*—a carefully designed environment for training believers to obey Jesus' commands. Believers got involved in church meetings through participatory meetings designed to stir up love and good deeds. Critical thinking skills were developed through discussion-styled teaching. Deep fellowship and solid relationships were fostered among disciples through the weekly celebration of the Lord's Supper as an actual meal. A strong commitment by the leaders to serve the church by building congregational consensus promoted unity. Disciple making in the context of these strategic church practices resulted in skyrocketing spiritual maturity.

Most importantly, the practices of the primitive church were clearly *scriptural*—a divine design. They were based on Jesus' teachings, instituted by the apostles, clearly practiced by first-century believers, and actually prescribed in the New Testament.[4] The strong relationships

---

[2]   EF Schumacher, "Small is Beautiful." *The Radical Humanist* Vol. 37, No. 5 (August 1973), 22.

[3]   Colossians 1:28.

[4]   2 Thessalonians 2:15, 1 Corinthians 14:37.

that grew out of these practices helped hold people in relational orbit during sometimes-difficult times of being disciplined. They constitute timeless and dynamic ecclesiological traditions for effectively making disciples of all nations.

Don't get the wrong idea. Simply adopting early small-church practice is not a substitute for the time-intensive task of intentional disciple making. However, if New Testament ecclesiology is followed, you can have a huge advantage in effectively teaching believers to obey all that Jesus commanded. According to David Platt, making disciples is what happens when we walk through life together, showing one another how to pray, study the Bible, grow in Christ, and lead others to Christ.[5] First-century ecclesiology can make your shepherding and disciple-making efforts infinitely more natural and effective:

> First-century church meetings were not a spectator sport. Any member could contribute verbally to the proceedings. The prime directive was that everything said had to be edifying, encouraging, equipping, or motivational. The leaders were more like side-line coaches than star players in this phase of the gathering.

> Their teaching times were characterized by dynamic discussions, not monologue sermons. This teaching style caused spiritual maturity and critical thinking skills to skyrocket.

> The Lord's Supper was celebrated every week, *as an actual meal.* It was a time of food, fellowship, community, one-another ministry, and building unity. This is where Hebrews 10:24-25 was lived out.

---

5   David Platt, "How Should We Be Making Disciples?" Radical.net. Accessed 08/30/2023.

The leaders' main authority lay in their ability to persuade with the truth. Rather than a top-down CEO model, church leaders took the time to serve the church by building congregational consensus on major decisions. This process strengthened the church and built unity.

Small churches that have adopted these New Testament strategies have abandoned the business model of church. They are more organic than organized, more family-like than corporate, smaller rather than larger, more relational than programmed, informal more than formal, focus more on one another than on one leader, and prefer authenticity over expertise. Additionally, first-century ecclesiology was designed to get far more people involved, making every member a minister. This spread-out ministry loads also took undue pressure off the bi-vocational leadership. Because genuine, close, solid relationships are developed through these practices, disciple making can be personalized—tailored to strengthen each person's weakness.

The leader of one of the first mega-churches frankly admitted that although his church attracted over 20,000 attendees weekly, they were not making disciples.[6] It's impossible to play baseball in a forest. You could play it on a football field, but it is much better to play it on an actual baseball field. So too with making disciples—the right small-church practices make an ideal playing field for effective shepherding.

In his book on God's will, Kevin DeYoung wrote, "Is there a better way to walk in the will of God? The answer is a resounding yes! There is most certainly a better way. It's an old way. It's a biblical way. It's Jesus' way."[7] Similarly, we ask, is there a better way to organize our churches? The answer is a resounding yes! There is most certainly a better way. It's an old way. It's a biblical way. It's Jesus' way. May the

---

6   Bob Burney, "Seeker Friendly Church Leader Admits They Have Done It All Wrong." ReformationHarvestFire.com. Accessed 06/22/2023.

7   Kevin DeYoung, *Just Do Something* (Chicago: Moody, 2009), 53.

Lord be pleased to greatly use you as part of His plan to "present the church to himself in splendor, without spot or wrinkle or any such thing, that she might be holy and without blemish."[8]

Stephen E. Atkerson
Atlanta, Georgia
2024

*The New Testament Reformation Fellowship (**NTRF.org**) is a teaching fellowship of small-church pastors helping other church leaders understand how to recapture the intimacy, simplicity, and dynamics of first-century church life. Frankly, we are not smart enough to dream up trendy new ways of doing church. However, we are smart enough to realize that, at least for us, it is best to stick with the tried-and-true examples left for us by the Twelve. You'll find free video, audio, and writings at NTRF.org. We are also available for consultations with other leaders (take advantage of our 30+ years of doing church this way!).*

---

[8] Ephesians 5:27.

Strategy #1

"Each One Has" Meetings To Stir Up Love & Good Deeds

How did Jesus and the Apostles design meetings of small churches so as to motivate believers to greater depths of faith and obedience? In their original design, church meetings were not a spectator sport. Considerable freedom was given congregants to address the church each week. There was a principle of participation. God's people were free to offer testimonies, share spiritual experiences, exhort, lead in prayer, testify to victory over sin, tell of God's grace in their lives, bring a new song, give praise to the Lord, etc. ("Let the redeemed of the Lord say so!").

Profit

The prime directive was that anything said had to be crafted to edify (strengthen, build up, encourage) the congregation. Another result was that love and good deeds were stirred up. Everything combined to motivate believers to greater obedience to the commands of the Lord, a key aspect of discipleship.

There are many other benefits to an open format. More people become actively involved in building up the church. The opportunity to make truly meaningful contributions to the meeting heightens congregational interest. The ideas that are shared tend to be practical, from the heart, and drawn from real-world applications of God's Word. All this not only takes a tremendous load off the leadership, but it allows them to enjoy being ministered to themselves. Furthermore, it prevents the development of apathy from frustration over passivity. There is a fuller expression of the spiritual gifts that involve speaking. This "open mic" approach also helps to avoid the atrophying of spiritual gifts from lack of use.

Professors

In the *Mid-America Baptist Theological Journal,* professor Jimmy Milikin stated that in early Christian congregations, "there was apparently a free expression of the Spirit. In the public assembly one person might have a psalm, another brother a teaching, another a revelation, another a tongue, another an interpretation."[1]

In *The Nature of the Early Church,* church historian Ernest Scott wrote: "The exercise of the spiritual gifts was thus the characteristic element in primitive worship. Those gifts might vary in their nature and degree according to the capacity of each individual, but they were bestowed on all and room was allowed in the service for the participation of all who were present.... Every member was expected to contribute something of his own to the common worship."[2]

In *Introducing the New Testament, theologian* John Drane wrote:

---

[1]   Jimmy Milikin, "Disorder Concerning Public Worship," *Mid-America Baptist Theological Journal* (Memphis: Mid-America Baptist Seminary Press, 1983), 125.

[2]   Ernest Scott, *The Nature of the Early Church* (New York: Charles Scribner's Sons, 1941), 79.

"In the earliest days … their worship was spontaneous. This seems to have been regarded as the ideal, for when Paul describes how a church meeting should proceed, he depicts a Spirit-led participation by many.… There was the fact that anyone had the freedom to participate in such worship. In the ideal situation, when everyone was inspired by the Holy Spirit, this was the perfect expression of Christian freedom."[3]

Concerning public worship in the New Testament church, London Bible College lecturer G.W. Kirby concluded: "There appears to have been considerable fluidity with time given for spontaneous participation."[4] Scottish commentator William Barclay stated: "The really notable thing about an early Church service must have been that almost everyone came feeling that he had both the privilege and obligation of contributing something to it."[5]

Proof

Synagogues

It is obvious from even a cursory reading of Acts that Paul was free to preach the Gospel in synagogues throughout the Roman world (Acts 13:14–15, 14:1, 17:1–2, 17:10, 18:4, 19:8). First-century synagogues were open to the participation of those in attendance. If the ancient synagogue meetings were in any way like modern Christian worship services, Paul would have needed a different strategy to spread the gospel to the Jews. Since Jewish Christians comprised the first churches, it is no wonder that the early church meetings were open to audience participation.[6]

---

[3] John Drane, *Introducing the New Testament* (Oxford, UK: Lion Publishing, 1999), 402.

[4] G. W. Kirby, *Zondervan Pictorial Encyclopedia of the Bible,* Vol. 1, ed. Merrell Tenney (Grand Rapids: Zondervan, 1982), 850.

[5] William Barclay, "Letters to the Corinthians," *Daily Study Bible* (Philadelphia: Westminster Press, 1977), 135.

[6] We do not advocate incorporating Jewish synagogue practices into the church. The point is simply that participatory meetings would not have been an unfamiliar idea to the earliest Christians.

Encourage One Another

A common text used to encourage church attendance is Hebrews 10:25 ("not neglecting to meet together"). The rest of the verse is just as important. The author of Hebrews also urged his readers (ordinary Christians) to "consider how to stir up one another to love and good works, not neglecting to meet together ... but encouraging one another" (Heb 10:24–25). Before coming to church, every believer was responsible for giving thought to how he might motivate others. It is clear that early church meetings were designed to provide ample opportunity for mutual encouragement. The focus was not exclusively on leaders; it was on "one another." Participatory meetings are in keeping with the principle of the fifty-nine "one another" Scripture passages (e.g., Jn 13:34; Ro 12:10; 1Pt 4:8; 1Jn 3:11, etc.). There was a principle of participation. It was about each member doing his part as led by the Spirit.[7] All members of Christ's body bore the responsibility to encourage the others through testimony, song, praise, prayer, exhortation, teaching, and the sharing of personal spiritual lessons learned.

Paul Talked With Them

Acts 20:7 records that Paul spoke all night when he visited the church at Troas. One Greek word that describes his actions is *dialegomai* (transliterated "dialogue"). It means to discuss.[8] In Acts 18:4 and 19:8, the same word is rendered as "reasoned" and "reasoning." The English Standard Version therefore states that Paul "talked with" them. Paul undoubtedly did most of the talking that night; however, it was not an uninterruptible sermon as if broadcast on the radio. Thus, the time that the early church set aside for teaching, even when led by an apostle, was to some degree discussion-oriented, another indicator that early church

---

[7] The Spirit's prompting is an essential element in participatory sharing; otherwise, it would be merely a religious version of amateur hour. Every believer has been given a spiritual gift to be used to build up the church, and the believer is to minister in accordance with this gifting. It is the duty of the leadership to equip the church to understand and practice this.

[8] Bauer, Arndt, Gingrich, *Greek-English Lexicon of the New Testament* (Chicago: Univ. of Chicago, 1979), 185.

meetings were characterized by a principle of participation.[9]

Each One Has

Guidelines for the use of spiritual gifts when "the whole church comes together" (1Co 14:23) are presented in 1 Corinthians 14. The *ESV Study Bible* states: "These verses give a fascinating glimpse into the kinds of activities that took place when the early church gathered as the body of Christ to worship the Lord."[10] This glimpse reveals a principle of participation: "What then, brothers? When you come together, each one has a hymn, a lesson, a revelation, a tongue, or an interpretation" (14:26). This text was directed to "each one" of the "brothers"—not just leaders. These early meetings were clearly not nearly as leader-centric as modern worship services. If the words "each one" (14:26) were replaced with "only one," which would better characterize your church services?

1 Corinthians 11–14 is a lengthy passage about church meetings. Amazingly, *leaders are not even mentioned in the entire section*. This does not mean that leaders are unimportant. On the contrary, they are critical to the proper functioning of a church. Thayer defined an *episcopos* as "one charged with the duty of seeing that things to be done are done rightly."[11] They are essential personnel. However, it appears that in the participatory phase of a church meeting, leaders are to be more like side-line coaches than star players.

New Testament believers did not merely *attend* services like spectators at a football game. "Each one" (14:26) of the brothers was free to use his verbal spiritual gifts to build up the gathered church. Ordinary believers were active, vital participants who could significantly contribute to what was said in the Sunday gathering.[12] The motto for these early church meetings could have been "every member a minister."

---

[9] Asking and allowing for questions and dialogue is good.

[10] Dennis & Grudem, eds., *ESV Study Bible* (Wheaton: Crossway Bibles, 2008), 2212.

[11] Joseph Thayer, *Greek–English Lexicon of the New Testament* (Grand Rapids: Baker Book House, 1977), 243.

[12] Not every person should be expected to say something at every gathering.

Edification

The overarching purpose for all that was said or done in such a gathering is edification: "Let all things be done for building up" (1Co 14:26). The Greek for "building up" (*oikodomé*) refers to the act of strengthening or encouraging. One lexicon has described *oikodomé* as the action of one who promotes another's growth in Christian wisdom, piety, and holiness.[13] Any comment made had to be lovingly designed to encourage, to build up, to strengthen, or to edify. If not, it was inappropriate and was to be left unspoken. The Corinthians were told, "Since you are eager for manifestations of the Spirit, strive to excel in building up the church" (1Co 14:12). Every testimony had to be well thought out so that it would build up the church. To be edifying, all teaching had to be both true and practicable. Prophecy served for "upbuilding and encouragement and consolation" (1Co 14:3).[14] Each person ministered according to his spiritual gifts. As Romans 12:6 says: "having gifts ... given to us, let us *use them*" (emphasis added). All this highlights the principle of participation in early church gatherings.

Music

The regulation of spiritual gifts related to singing is addressed in 1 Corinthians 14. Thus, when Paul wrote that "each one" had a "hymn" (*psalmos*, 14:26), he meant each one gifted in music. Musicians in good standing with the church had the freedom to edify the congregation through this gift. Those with musical gifts should facilitate the entire church's singing: "the music must not turn the church into an audience enjoying the music, but into a congregation singing the Lord's praises in His presence."[15] Our music should reflect the Psalmist's invitation: "Let us come into his presence with thanksgiving; let us make a joyful noise to him with songs of praise!" (Ps 95:2).

---

[13] Thayer, *Lexicon*, 40.

[14] Even convicting reproof can be edifying.

[15] D. A. Carson, ed., *Worship by the Book* (Grand Rapids: Zondervan, 2010), 212.

The early church's singing also had a "one another" aspect. All believers, even those who were not musically gifted were admonished: "be filled with the Spirit, addressing one another in psalms and hymns and spiritual songs, singing and making melody to the Lord with your heart" (Eph 5:19). Similarly, the Colossian believers were exhorted to "[admonish] one another with psalms and hymns and spiritual songs, singing with thankfulness in your hearts to God" (Col 3:16). Thus, it appears that there was a principle of participation in their music.

Teaching

In-depth biblical exposition, with clear application, was an integral part of each weekly church meeting. Church leaders rightly do most of the teaching on the Lord's Day. However, the New Testament says that "each one" of the brothers who had the gift of teaching also had the freedom to bring the weekly "lesson" (1Co 14:26). Thus, James cautioned: "not many of you should become teachers, my brothers, for you know that we who teach will be judged with greater strictness" (Jm 3:1). This caution makes sense in light of the participatory meetings that characterized the early church. In accordance with the principle of participation, there was clearly an opportunity for supernaturally gifted, mature brothers to teach (with pastoral approval and coaching).[16] (In another chapter, evidence is presented that first-century teaching times were more discussion than lecture).

Two or Three Tongues

The participatory nature of early church meetings is also evident in the guidelines for those who spoke in tongues: "If any speak in a tongue, let there be only two or at most three, and each in turn, and let someone interpret. But if there is no one to interpret, let each of them keep silent in church and speak to himself and to God" (1Co 14:27–28).

---

[16] 1 Timothy 2:12 prohibits women from teaching Scripture to men, so only brothers should bring the lessons.

Interpretation was required "so that the church might be built up" (1Co 14:5). Multiple people participated, one at a time, and there was clearly a degree of spontaneity. Many have judged the gift of tongues to be a phenomenon limited to the first century.[17] Even if tongues have ceased, the overall principle of spontaneous participation remains. Congregants could still contribute through teaching, song, testimony, prayer, exhortation, encouragement, and public Scripture reading.

Two or Three Prophets

The participatory nature of New Testament gatherings is also seen in the guidelines for first-century prophecy: "Let two or three prophets speak, and let the others weigh what is said" (1Co 14:29). The impromptu nature of prophecy is clear: "If a revelation is made to another sitting there, let the first be silent" (1Co 14:30). The goal of prophecy was "that all may learn and all be encouraged" (1Co 14:31). It is the studied conviction of many that the gift of prophecy, like tongues, ceased with the apostolic age.[18] Even so, a principle of participation remains. It is the leaders' duty to be sure that everything is done "decently and in order" (1Co 14:40).

Women To Be Silent

Scripture states that "women should keep silent in the churches" (1Co 14:33b). This command is irrelevant in most of today's churches because generally no one, *man or woman*, except leaders, speaks. Whatever this prohibition meant, it would not have been written unless first-century church meetings were participatory. Thus, even this prohibition reflects the principle of participation.

---

[17] Were all charismatic churches to follow the guidelines of 1 Corinthians 14 (a maximum of three, one at a time, must be interpreted), much of what passes for legitimate tongues would be deemed out of order.

[18] It is the leaders' job to save the church from needless vexation by the emotionally unstable who fancy themselves prophets and would give weekly warnings of an atomic holocaust.

Perspective

It is helpful to have a good perspective on why participatory sharing is important, and how it was lost. After Theodosius made Christianity the official religion of the Roman Empire (A.D. 380), large pagan temples were often repurposed as church buildings. Church gatherings moved from the relative intimacy of Roman villas to vast, impersonal basilicas. These large church services naturally morphed into performances by professionals. Dialogical teaching gave way to eloquent monologues. Spontaneity was lost, and with it, the principle of participation. The "one another" aspect of assembly became impractical. "Each one has" became "only one has." Informality was transformed into formality. Church leaders began to wear special clerical costumes. Worship aids, such as incense, icons, candles, and hand gestures, were introduced. In *A Lion Handbook—The History of Christianity,* Church of Scotland minister Henry Sefton, wrote: "Worship in the house-church had been of an intimate kind in which all present had taken an active part ... (this) changed from being 'a corporate action of the whole church' into 'a service said by the clergy to which the laity listened.'"[19]

Many consider traditional worship services to be participatory simply because the congregation joins in responsive readings, partakes of the Lord's Supper, enjoys congregational singing, and gives financial offerings. These are positive aspects of worship; however, they do not constitute an open format. Gordon Fee observed, "By and large, the history of the church points to the fact that in worship we do not greatly trust the diversity of the body. Edification must always be the rule, and that carries with it orderliness so that all may learn and all be encouraged. But it is no great credit to the historical church that in opting for 'order' it also opted for a silencing of the ministry of the many."[20]

---

[19]   Henry Sefton, *A Lion Handbook —The History of Christianity* (Oxford, UK: Lion Publishing, 1988), 151.

[20]   Gordon Fee, "The First Epistle to the Corinthians," *New International Commentary on the New Testament* (Grand Rapids: Eerdmans, 1987), 698.

Instead of couch potatoes, we have trained God's people to be pew potatoes. Many feel that they might as well stay home and watch church on television. Not allowing the ministry of the many can cause apathy, as illustrated in the joke about a Sunday school teacher who once asked the children, "Why must we be quiet in church?" One perceptive little girl replied, "Because people are sleeping in there."

The verbal participation of the members makes for a greater working of the Spirit because it allows the many gifts of the ministry to flourish. According to Paul's writings in 1 Corinthians 14, God might burden a number of believers, independently of one another, to bring a short testimony or word of encouragement, to lead out in prayer, or to bring a song. Additional applications and illustrations can be offered by the body at large to augment a word of instruction. Congregants could ask questions or make comments during or after the teaching time. New believers learn how to think with the mind of Christ as they observe the more mature believers share in the meeting. Maturity will greatly increase. The brothers will begin to own the meeting. They will take responsibility for the flow of the meeting as they become active participants rather than passive spectators. Edification is thus accomplished.

Proposition

After providing guidelines for the use of tongues and prophecy in participatory sharing, Paul concluded, "The things I am writing to you are a command of the Lord" (1Co 14:37). A command is not a suggestion. It is more than a good idea. The instructions in 1 Corinthians 14 are not merely interesting history. These participatory regulations for tongues and prophecy were not just descriptions of primitive church meetings. In some sense, they were prescriptive. The Lord's command assumes a greater context of open participation by the many.

Our proposition is that you consider introducing participatory sharing to your church. Perhaps you fear it is not worth the anticipated problems it might create. We would point out that where there are no oxen, the manger is clean, but much increase comes from their strength (Pr 14:4). The potential blessing is worth the risk. Remember the seven last words of declining churches: "We never did it that way before."

Some in Corinth wanted to conduct their meetings differently from the requirements set forth in 1 Corinthians 14. They were asked two questions: "Or was it from you that the word of God came? Or are you the only ones it has reached?" (1Co 14:36). The word of God clearly did not originate with the Corinthians, and they most certainly were not the only people whom it had reached. (As such, whatever applied to the Corinthian church would also apply to us.) These questions were designed to convince the Corinthian believers that they had no authority to conduct their meetings in any other way than that prescribed by the apostles. The principle of participation was to be observed.

Should the time when the body comes together be focused mostly on church leaders, or is it an opportunity for God to speak through multiple saints to those gathered? Broadening the focus to include the messages of multiple people strengthens the church as a whole. The church is thus not as dependent on the gifts of one man. Often, when a gifted leader leaves a church, attendance plummets. The likelihood of the development of a personality cult is lessened. One of Martin Luther's arguments for reformation concerned the priesthood of all believers. Do we really believe in the priesthood of the believer? If so, perhaps we could prove it by allowing the priests to minister during our gatherings. In church meetings designed by Jesus and the apostles, there was the freedom to speak (the person did have to be a church leader)—an open format for sharing/testimony. There was a free exercise of spiritual gifts that involved speaking. Verbal contributions to the meeting were the norm. The expectation was that believers would come prepared for an "each one has" meeting. This resulted in the open, Spirit-led participation by the many. The incentive for people to aspire to greater depths of discipleship is tremendous.

Practicum

Leadership's Role

Church leaders who are new to the idea of participatory meetings are wisely cautious. With good reason, they anticipate unedifying scenarios. One of a leader's roles is to keep church meetings on track in order to be true to the prime directive that all things be edifying. Lexicographer Joseph Thayer defined an *episcopos* as "a man charged with the duty of seeing that things to be done by others are done rightly."[21] He described a *presbutéros* as one who "presided over the assemblies."[22] If a meeting is not edifying, the leaders are responsible for making the necessary adjustments.

Ephesians 4:11–12 reveals that it is the duty of pastor-teachers to equip the saints for ministry. This includes training that prepares them to make meaningful contributions in a participatory meeting. If the Scriptures truly reveal God's desire for participatory meetings to be held, then we can expect God to work through the leaders to see that the meetings are successful. There is order in a cemetery; however, there is no life. It is much better to risk a little disorder to have life. The Holy Spirit must be trusted to work in the life of a church.

Edifying participatory church meetings do not "just" happen. New Testament-styled participatory gatherings are to be Spirit led, and the Spirit works through leaders to make it edifying. They are behind-the-scenes coaches, encouraging and training so that everyone ministers in accordance with his spiritual gifts and everything that is said is edifying.

Baby Steps

Start slowly. Do not initially try to have fully participatory meetings. Instead, during the week, if you hear a brother share something that the Lord taught him, enlist him to share it in church the following

---

21   Thayer, *Lexicon*, 243.
22   Thayer, *Lexicon*, 536.

Sunday. Work with him to make sure that it is short (no more than seven minutes) and practicable. Coach him to ensure brevity and clarity. Each week, a few brothers could be scheduled to share a short testimony in the meeting. A person who shares a witnessing experience can motivate the timid to evangelism. A testimony about a need met or a prayer answered in God's providence can encourage others who are going through hard times. A person who is involved in a jail ministry can talk about good results with inmates and induce others to get involved. Real-life stories with a spiritual emphasis are very uplifting. The congregation will thus become accustomed to greater participation and have a model for the appropriate type of edifying sharing. As the congregation grows accustomed to this approach, the total time allotted for sharing can be increased, and those who are moved by the Spirit can be given more latitude to rise from their seats to share without having been scheduled to speak.

Cultural Resistance

In the West, to have participatory instead of performance-type church meetings is countercultural. Many will find participatory sharing uncomfortable. One Baptist church that experimented with it on Sunday nights suffered a precipitous decline in attendance at that service. (Some complained that they did not want to hear amateurs' opinions; they wanted to hear polished presentations by professional pastors.) Teaching, training, and equipping by leadership are necessary for God's people to be prepared for participation. The typical church member is not a professional speaker; thus, the potential for imperfect presentations is ever present. However, "love bears all things" (1Co 13:7). If participatory meetings are truly Christ's desire, then it is ultimately immaterial how strange it seems in our culture. As with the pearl of great price, the benefit is worth the cost. People will become more open to participatory meetings after they are taught obedience to God's Word and understand that it is a scriptural concept.

Sound Barrier

After years of passively attending services, most Christians are conditioned to sit silent in church as if watching television. Patient encouragement is necessary to overcome this. Meaningful participation will seem awkward to people initially. Continual encouragement by the leadership may be necessary until the "sound barrier" is broken. During the week, leaders should work behind the scenes to encourage the brethren to share. Asking men to lead weekly prayer or public reading of Scripture can help them to overcome their reticence.

Open participation does not preclude private preparation. Every brother should be coached to consider *in advance* how the Lord might have him edify the church (Heb 10:25). If a string were stretched across the surface of a stream, various things that would otherwise have floated past would become attached to it as the day progressed. Similarly, thinking all week long about what to bring to the next meeting helps greatly. If no one brought food to a family reunion, there would not be much of a feast. If no one comes to participatory gatherings prepared to contribute, there will not be much sharing.

The following could be asked of the brothers: *What has the Lord shown you this week during your time with Him? Is there a testimony the Lord would have you bring? Could you commit to begin a time of conversational prayer? Is there a song that would edify the church? Is there a subject or passage of Scripture to teach on? Did you have victory over sin this week? What work of grace did God do in your life?*

The worst cause of a lack of participation is the absence of anything spiritual to share. Many Christians are neither walking with the Lord nor living Spirit-filled lives. They are as straight as a gun barrel theologically, and just as empty. Such spiritually-dull believers will have little that is worthwhile to share on Sunday. Edifying participatory meetings happen only when church members abide in Jesus. Too often, liturgy and clerical dominance become a necessary cover for congregational carnality. In contrast, genuine heartfelt sharing and confession in the meeting can cause those living lives of hypocrisy to come under conviction and repent of their sin. Obedience is contagious! People who love Jesus do not come to church to worship; they bring their worship with them.

Unedifying Remarks

Sometimes, after brothers have grown accustomed to sharing, they become overly casual in their remarks. Spontaneous utterances often do not edify the assembly. An open format does not mean that people can say anything they want to say. Leaders need to remind the church that whatever is said in the meeting must be designed to build up the body. Sometimes, merely requiring speakers to rise and stand behind a pulpit, lectern, or music stand at the front of the room (as opposed to speaking from their seats) will effectively squelch casual, unedifying remarks. The leaders must coach each person to remember: "A word fitly spoken is like apples of gold in a setting of silver" (Pr 25:11).

Church meetings must not become therapy sessions for the wounded. The focus should not be exclusively on needy persons. If allowed, spiritual black holes can suck the life out of the meeting. Such people do need counseling; however, it should be done at a time other than during the church meeting. Corporate edification must remain the prime directive.

It is the leaderships' responsibility to help people understand what is and is not edifying and to provide private coaching to help people to make only edifying comments. Brothers should be trained to tell what the time is rather than how to build a clock. As does a pencil, every message should have a point. Those who share should also be taught to focus on one point to keep it short. The words spoken must have power. The goal must be exhortation. Despite the best modeling, some brothers simply will not "get it"; they need private and repeated coaching regarding edifying versus unedifying comments.

There is to be a certain degree of decorum. Peter said, "As each has received a gift, use it to serve one another, as good stewards of God's varied grace: whoever speaks, as one who speaks oracles of God" (1Pe 4:10–11). Participatory church meetings should not be interactive. It is generally not edifying when someone in the audience tries to interact with the person who was burdened to stand up to share. The church should not be subjected to having to listen to a public conversation. To edify the church during the sharing time, individuals should present verbal offerings with the same attitude in which the Old Testament saints brought offerings. Others should be discouraged from piling on or adding to something that has already been offered (we call it dieseling).

Aberrant Theology

The lure of a participatory meeting might attract those looking to promote an eccentric doctrine. This is another situation where leaders are needed. Timothy, stationed in Ephesus and temporarily functioning as an elder, was to "charge certain persons not to teach any different doctrine" (1Ti 1:3). One qualification for an elder is that he must "be able to give instruction in sound doctrine and also to rebuke those who contradict it" (Titus 1:9). Similarly, Titus was told: "Exhort and rebuke with all authority. Let no one disregard you" (Titus 2:15). John warned about a known deceiver: "Do not receive him into your house" (2Jn 1:10).[23] The prevention and correction of error is one reason elders are needed.

One way to filter out doctrinal error is for the church to have an official statement of faith. Remarks made during the church meeting must be consistent with the belief statement. Members with odd beliefs should not be free to publicly express them. In addition, only brothers who are in good standing with the church should be allowed to share. Each week, an announcement should be made that only church members are permitted to speak. The leaders are the gatekeepers for would-be speakers.

---

[23] John's instructions were especially relevant to house churches with participatory meetings.

Pooled Ignorance

During an interview on participatory gatherings, a Christian radio broadcaster astutely asked, "How do you keep the guy who knows the least from saying the most?" Rather than considering in advance how to encourage the church, some will come to the meeting unprepared. People who are socially clueless and lacking the Spirit's direction will make impromptu, rambling, repetitive speeches that would be better left unsaid. It is the leaders' job to know the congregation well enough to be aware of those who are likely to do excessive and inappropriate sharing. They must work with them to help them to be informed, concise, and judicious in their sharing.

Congregational Size

Meetings that are either too big (hundreds of people) or too small (fewer than ten or twenty) present hindrances to participation. The presence of too many people will be inimical to intimacy. It will intimidate the shy and inhibit sharing and accountability. Only a tiny fraction of those present in a big meeting would be able to share anyway (even if they had the courage). Too few contributions from people in a tiny congregation could make the meeting seem dull because of the absence of diversity of spiritual gifts. The typical first-century church, meeting in a wealthy person's villa, might have sixty-five to seventy people in attendance.[24] There were 120 in the upper room.[25] Early church meetings comprised scores of people: not hundreds and, certainly, not thousands.

One home-field advantage for small churches is the possibility of having truly edifying participatory church experiences. When well-managed by leaders, open participation taps into the congregation's spiritual gifts. People become excited about attending because they can make meaningful contributions and be blessed by those of

---

[24] Graydon Snyder, *Church Life Before Constantine* (Macon, GA: Mercer University Press, 1991), 70.

[25] Acts 1:15 may not reflect a normal church meeting; however, it indicates the number of people who could assemble in a first-century room.

others. Sometimes, a complete message from God is conveyed through the beautiful blending of testimonies, teaching, songs, and encouragement of multiple people (many springs flowing into one river). The promotion of "one anothering" in the assembly can be of great encouragement to those involved with small churches. Why would Scripture speak of these things if they were not important? Participatory sharing can transform small church meetings from ordinary to extraordinary.

Latecomers

If a brother is earnestly sharing from his heart when a late-arriving family suddenly bursts into the meeting, everyone will naturally turn to see who is entering. The late-comers then climb over people who are already seated, chairs are shuffled, etc. What effect would this have on the message that was being shared? It will be disrupted, and the Spirit will be squelched. Late arrivals should be asked to wait quietly outside. They should not enter the meeting area until a song is being sung or there is a change of speakers.

In participatory meetings, it is not unusual for a latecomer to request a song that has already been sung. Even worse, a late brother might bring an exhortation related to a current event that the church had already spent several minutes considering. The church could adopt a policy that requires late arrivals to refrain from speaking because they would not know what has already transpired (it will also discourage tardiness).

So Little Time

Incorporating music, participatory sharing, and an in-depth lesson will be difficult in a meeting that is limited to one hour. A one-and-a-half or two-hour meeting would be more ideal; even then, the meeting must be carefully managed. Attention should be paid to the time designated for each phase of the meeting (singing, sharing, and teaching). In addition, limits should be placed on the number of people who can share and the amount of time allotted to each person. Re-marks could be limited to 5 to 7 minutes. This will prevent the meeting from being dominated by one person and thus allow multiple people to share. It will be necessary for the leadership to occasionally interrupt long-winded speakers. (A sample bulletin is provided below).

In-Depth Bible Teaching

Feeding the sheep is a critical component of healthy church life. Quality, in-depth teaching that is geared to believers should be an integral part of each Sunday church meeting. This is the "lesson" that is referred to in 1 Corinthians 14:26. Our Lord instructed the apostles to make disciples by *teaching* obedience to His commandments (Mt 28:20). The Jerusalem church was devoted to the apostles' *teaching* (Acts 2:42). One requirement for an elder is that he have the ability to *teach* (1Ti 3:2). Elders who work hard at teaching are declared worthy of financial support (1Ti 5:17–18). Thus, the importance of teaching should not be underestimated. The ideal is a steady diet of the sys-tematic exposition of Scripture with clear, practical application. If the "what" (content) does not lead to "so what" (application), then the "what" has not been taught correctly. The goal of all instruction should be to promote love from a pure heart, a good conscience, and sincere faith (1Ti 1:5).

Because we want people to come to Christ, we can be tempted to convert church meetings into evangelistic services. However, the New Testament indicates that church gatherings are primarily for the benefit of believers. Church meetings are to build Christians up in their faith, and to encourage obedience. So important is teaching, that if one had to choose between a church that had participatory meetings but no in-depth teaching, and one that had good teaching but was not partici-patory, we would advise picking the church with in-depth exposition.[26]

---

[26] We advise this based on thirty-plus years of experience with participatory meetings.

Charismatic Gifts

Churches that promote the exercise of charismatic gifts must ensure that the guidelines in 1 Corinthians 14:26–32 are followed closely. Speaking in tongues is not to be allowed unless it can be interpreted. A maximum of three tongue speakers should be allowed. Prophecies should also be limited to three speakers. Anyone who prophesies must realize that his words will be weighed carefully and judged. Managing this can be confusing and frustrating because the overly emotional and unstable often imagine they have such gifts. Perhaps that is why the Thessalonians were given this admonition: "Do not treat prophecies with contempt. Test everything. Hold on to the good. Avoid every kind of evil" (1Th 5:20–22). In the midst of these supernatural utterances, there must be order: "The spirits of the prophets are subject to the control of the prophets. God is not a God of disorder but of peace" (1Co 14:32-33a). Here again, the leaders played a key role in ensuring that everything was done in a "fitting and orderly way" (1Co 14:40). Leaders are responsible for quality control.

Women

A principle of participation obviously does not mean "anything goes." Those who spoke in tongues had to be silent if there was no interpreter. Prophets had to be silent if interrupted. In each case, restraint was required for the greater good. Paul's first letter to Timothy (1Ti 2:12) reveals that women are not to teach or have authority over men. Thus, sisters are not free to present the lesson (1Co 14:26). 1 Corinthians 14:33b–35 appears to further limit their participation (see NTRF.org for help with this topic).[27]

Children

The New Testament indicates that children were present with their parents in church meetings. For example, Paul intended some of

---

[27] "Women: Silent in Church?"

his letters to be read aloud to the entire church (Col 4:16). Had children not been present in the meeting, they would not have heard Paul's instruction to them (Eph 6:1–3; see also Mt 19:13–15; Lk 2:41–50; Acts 21:5). It is better for children to remain with their parents in worship rather than to be segregated in a children's church.

A young child who begins to cry loudly in the meeting should be removed by a parent until he has been quieted. Having a room designated for this purpose is beneficial. Some parents will be oblivious to this need. In such cases, the leadership must speak to the parents in private to enlist their cooperation in controlling their children. Older children should be taught to sit still or to play silently on the floor to avoid being disruptive.

False Expectations

New people will invariably come to a participatory church meeting with preconceived notions. For example, some will want to have an emotional worship experience or to sing only the great hymns of the faith. Others will exclusively associate praise songs with heartfelt worship, expect dramatic healings to take place, or desire a tear-jerking presentation of the Gospel. When their expectations are not met, disappointment and discontent are the result. Church leaders need to be aware of this and take steps to help people to have biblical expectations of the meetings. For example, a description of a typical church meeting could be posted on the church website. During each meeting, a brief statement could be made about the way that the church meeting will be conducted, or a bulletin could be provided to visitors so that they would know what to expect.

Regenerate Membership

The ability to have participatory church meetings requires a regenerate church membership. Reformers felt that one of the characteristics of a true church was church discipline.[28] The wonder of the gospel is that provision is made for the sinning brother who cannot find his way to repentance on his own. The grace of a loving congregation will help him be restored to full fellowship.[29]

Three Phases

We recommend three phases for every Lord's Day meeting. The first phase might be participatory: singing, public Scripture reading, testimonies, and praying, followed by a short break. The second phase could be the dialogical lesson. The third phase would be the Lord's Supper/*Agapé*. Of course, the order of the phases could be changed to meet the needs of the fellowship.

Sample Bulletin

10:15–10:30 Arrive & Settle In

Meet people, enjoy a cup of coffee, and find a seat.

10:30–11:30 Song & Testimony

First-century church meetings were characterized by "each one has" (1Co 14:26). Accordingly, believers in good standing with the church are free to use their spiritual gifts to build up the gathered saints through songs, short testimonies, Scripture readings, exhortations, or praise.

11:30–11:45 Short Break

Stand up, stretch your legs, refresh your coffee, and fellowship.

11:45–12:30 Bible Discussion

An integral part of our participatory gathering is the in-depth, dialogical teaching of God's Word.

---

[28] *Belgic Confession*, Article 29.
[29] Matthew 18:15-22.

12:30–2:30 Lords' Supper/Agapé Feast

The early church celebrated the Lord's Supper weekly as a literal meal. This holy meal is a wonderful time of edification through fellowship. Central are the cup and loaf, which symbolize Jesus' death on the cross to pay for our sins. The single cup and single loaf symbolize unity. An enacted prayer, the Lord's Supper reminds us of Jesus' promise to return and eat it again with us at the Wedding Banquet of the Lamb. Come, Lord Jesus!

Discussion Questions

1. Taken as a whole, what statements in 1 Corinthians 14 indicate that early church meetings were participatory?

2. Suppose 1 Corinthians 14:26 is a criticism of the Corinthian church. What is the significance of the inspired solution being a regulation of participation rather than a prohibition of participation?

3. Why is it important for everything that is said in the church meeting to be edifying? *See 1 Corinthians 14:1–25.*

4. According to 1 Corinthians 14 and Hebrews 10:24–25, what are some of the guiding principles for participatory church meetings?

5. What role should leaders play in participatory meetings? *See 1 Timothy 1:3–5, 3:5, 4:11–14, 5:17, 6:2b; 2 Timothy 4:1–2; Titus 2:1, 2:15.*

6. What can be done if, week after week, few saints share anything of significance in participatory meetings?

7. Why would the absence of charismatic gifts not nullify the general principle of participatory church meetings?

8. What is the Lord commanding in 1 Corinthians 14:37?

9. According to Acts 2:42, Acts 14:26–28, and 1 Timothy 4:13, what are some appropriate contributions to a church meeting?

10. What advantages does a smaller congregation have over a larger one regarding participatory gatherings?

NTRF.org has audio, video, articles, and a teacher's discussion guide on participatory church meetings.

Strategy #2

Maturing the Saints Through Dialogical Teaching

Much good comes from preaching in large churches (such as done by Charles Spurgeon). However, in smaller congregations the opportunity cost of monologue presentations should be considered. *What teaching method does the New Testament offer for effectively making disciples in fellowships of under 100?*

Profit

A major advantage of adopting a dialogical teaching style for bi-vocational pastors is the time saved in sermon preparation. Since there is discussion involved, not as much text can be covered each week (but what is covered will be better grasped by the church), so not as much time will need to be spent on weekly research. Furthermore, the message does not have to be crafted into a monologue performance (three points and a poem), also saving time.

Opportunity Costs

A friend asked ChatGPT, "What are the overall opportunity costs of monologue presentations?" This was the response: "The overall opportunity costs of monologue presentations include the time and resources spent preparing for the presentation, the potential for a lack of audience engagement, and the inability to benefit from feedback or collaboration. Additionally, monologue presentations can be less effective than interactive presentations in terms of conveying information and inspiring action."

An Inferior Teaching Method

A monologue presentation is, frankly, an inferior method for causing learning in smaller congregations. This is because many listeners have a limited concentration span (typically twenty minutes). Consequently, they tune in and out, only grasping fragments of a lecture, and quickly forget the rest. Worst yet, a weekly diet of sermons, "apes one of the worst features of modern industrial society—the creation of a dependent, unreflective, semi-literate, relatively skill-less population, almost devoid of creativity. Far from realizing that the stimulation of other minds is one of the chief duties of a teacher, most preachers often do the exact opposite."[1]

Participatory Pedagogy

For the first several centuries of its existence, Christianity was an illegal religion. Churches had to meet secretly, usually in private homes. Perhaps as many as one hundred people might squeeze into a Roman villa, but not hundreds and certainly not thousands. In such small congregations, was the preaching of one-way, monologue sermons *de rigeur?*

---

[1]   David C Norrington, *To Preach or Not to Preach?* (Omaha: Ekklesia Press, 1996), 125.

Paul Talked With Them

Consider the words Luke used to describe how Paul taught when visiting the church in Troas (Acts 20:7ff). First, Luke recorded that "Paul <u>talked with</u> them" (20:7), from *dielegeto*, the lexical form of which is *dialégomai* (transliterated "dialogue"). It's primary meaning is "to conduct a discussion."[2] In other places, *dialégomai* is rendered as "reasoned" and "reasoning."[3] Next, Luke noted that Paul "prolonged his <u>speech</u> until midnight" (20:7). "Speech" is from *logos*, a very broad term. Although it certainly can refer to a speech, *logos* can also simply mean speaking as in talking.[4]

Paul Conversed With Them

Luke further described Paul's method of communication by writing that Paul "<u>conversed</u> with them a long while." (20:11). In English, the word converse is obviously related to conversation. The underlying Greek is *homileo*, "to speak with someone."[5] In this passage, *homileo* is a virtual synonym with *dialégomai*. Paul doubtless had much to say, but based on Acts 20:7-11, it appears that he did not deliver the information in the form of a lecture. Paul's teaching method was clearly more of a discussion than a monologue. It certainly was not an *uninterruptible* message as if broadcast on the radio.

One Another

Early church meetings were quite intimate, allowing for great emphasis on "one another" ministry. For example, Hebrews 10:24-25 exhorts ordinary believers not to forsake the assembly, but instead to "stir <u>one another</u> up to love and good works ... encouraging <u>one another</u>." Colossians 3:16 states that believers are to be "teaching and admonishing <u>one another</u>." Paul was satisfied that Christians in Rome were "able to

---

2   Bauer, *Lexicon*, 185.
3   Acts 18:4 and 19:8
4   Bauer, *Lexicon,* 477.
5   Bauer, *Lexicon*, 565.

instruct <u>one another</u>" (Ro 15:14). A more interactive style of teaching would seem more fitting in the context of a "one another" approach to church meetings.

Participation

It is obvious from 1 Corinthians 14 that spontaneity, informality, and the freedom for ordinary, non-ordained members to speak was the norm in New Testament church meetings: "when you come together, *each one has* ..." (14:26, italics mine). The guidelines were that only one at a time could speak, and that anything said had to be intended to build up the church. All of this orderly participation was declared to be "a command of the Lord" (14:37). In this "each one has" context, Paul also referenced a "lesson" (ESV; from *didaché*; transliterated "didactic," 14:26). The NIV here has "a word of instruction" and the NASV has "teaching"—*none of the three translated it as "preaching."* With such an open format, how likely was it that the congregation was required to sit mutely and passively listen to a one-way lecture?

Learn Quietly

Paul prohibited women from teaching or having authority over a man. Instead, women were to learn "quietly with all submissiveness" (1 Tim 2:11). The Greek for "quietly" (*heschuia*) primarily means quiet in the sense of not causing trouble, of not wrangling with the teacher. It was used earlier in 1 Timothy 2:1-2 wherein prayers were urged for kings so that Christians "may lead a peaceful and quiet (*heschuia*) life." It was also used in 2 Thessalonians 3:11-12 with reference to idle busybodies who were encouraged "to do their work quietly (*heschuia*) and to earn their own living." Thus, during teaching times, women were to be settled down, not disputing with the teacher—a requirement that need not have been stated unless it was common for congregants to interact with the speaker.

Early Christian History

A study of early Christian historical writings confirms that the lessons in church meetings were of such a nature that there was considerable frankness and openness between teacher and the congregation. Speakers were interrupted by such things as clapping, the foot stomping, suggestions to the speaker, the public congregational quoting of Scripture, crying, laughing, and dialogue between speaker and the audience.[6] It was far from the situation today where congregants sit quietly, and passively listen to a high-powered Bible lecture.

Professors

One skill that many educators continue to find difficult to teach is critical thinking. The philosopher Socrates noticed positively that his disciples often lost the ability to justify their own preconceived beliefs after facing a series of specific, targeted questions. Therefore, using further appropriate questioning, Socrates discovered that these same students eventually developed self-generated knowledge and the ability to regulate their own thoughts.[7]

100 Recorded Questions by Jesus

Teaching for critical thinking is a rational and intentional act.[8] It simply cannot be taught in a church where the pastor always lectures. According to D.A. Blight, an expert on teaching methods, "… if students are to learn to think, they must be placed in situations where they have to do so. The situations in which they are obliged to think are those in which they have to answer questions because questions demand an active response…."[9] Thus, it should not come as a surprise that asking questions made up the core of Jesus' teaching method in

---

6   Norrington, *Preach*, 35.

7   Douglas Oyler & Frank Romanelli, *The Fact of Ignorance: Revisiting the Socratic Method as a Tool for Teaching Critical Thinking.* ncbi.nlm.nih.gov. Accessed 09/07/2023.

8   "Critical Thinking Skills Toolkit", ADEA.org. Accessed 11/21/2023.

9   Norrington, *Preach*, 124.

smaller settings. There are over 100 recorded questions asked by Jesus in the Gospels. He was constantly asking questions (and it wasn't because He didn't know the answer!). It has been said that Jesus "came not to answer questions, but to ask them; not to settle men's souls, but to provoke them."[10]

Bad Habits

Habits of students who do *not* use critical thinking skills include disorganization in thought processing and preparation, overly simplistic thinking ("I have enough information. There is no need to seek additional information."), and the use of unreasonable criteria ("I prayed about it, and my belief is sincere. Evidence to the contrary is irrelevant.").[11]

Good Habits

Educator Robert Ennis summarized that critical thinkers tend to be capable of both adopting and changing a position as evidence dictates, can remain relevant to the point, seek information, remain open minded, take the entire situation into account, be able to keep the original problem in mind, search for reasons, deal with the components of a complex problem in an orderly manner, seek a clear statement of the problem, look for options, exhibit sensitivity to others' feelings and depth of knowledge, and use credible sources.[12]

Preaching Vs. Teaching

One major difference between preaching and teaching in modern thinking is that a teaching can more naturally be interrupted. Questions can be asked, insights added, and disagreements stated. Jesus commissioned the apostles with the making of disciples, a process that He

---

[10]   HH Horne, *Jesus the Master Teacher* (New York: Association Press, 1920), 51.

[11]   "Critical Thinking Skills Toolkit", ADEA.org. Accessed 11/21/2023.

[12]   Robert Ennis, "Critical thinking and subject specificity: clarification and needed research", *Educ Researcher 1989*; 18: 4-10.

said required "teaching" (*didasko*) people to do all that He commanded—*not preaching about doing it.*[13] Acts 2:42 makes it clear that the
disciples were devoted to the Apostles' "teaching" (*didaché*)—not their
preaching. In sync with this, in the two passages that cite qualifications
for a church leader, one states that he must be "able to teach (*didatikos*)"
(1Ti 3:2), and the other, "able to give instruction (*didaskalia*)" (Titus
1:9). *The ability to preach was not a requirement.* In 2 Timothy 2:24-25a,
we learn that the Lord's servant must be "able to teach … correcting his
opponents with gentleness" (this gentle teaching approach would seem
to be the opposite of one way, performance-style preaching).

Virtuoso Skill Set

Compounding the problem is the fact that few church leaders
have the considerable virtuoso skill set necessary to effectively craft and
deliver an interesting lecture. Perhaps worst yet, one-way communication too often blunts curiosity, causes passivity, creates an unhealthy
dependence on the preacher, and does not effectively equip people for
independent study. Lecturing is an unnatural, inappropriate, less-effec-
tive, overly-formal method of communicating in small churches.

Preaching's Pedigree

In secular Greek and Roman society an oratorical style known
as rhetoric was a popular form of entertainment. It was very similar to
what we today think of as preaching. It was an interesting, persuasive,
emotionally-moving, monologue performance. It was even regarded as
an art form.[14]

Huge Buildings, Large Numbers

Historians such as Edwin Hatch inform us that it was not until
centuries after the New Testament era that monologue rhetoric was

---

[13] Matthew 28:19-20.
[14] Norrington, *Preach*, 44.

regularly incorporated into church meetings.[15] Its introduction was due in part to the sudden influx of large numbers of nominal believers into the church after Christianity was made the Empire's official religion. Furthermore, congregations moved from the intimacy of privately-owned Roman villas into large, impersonal buildings that could accommodate hundreds.[16]

Nominal Believers

The "one another," discussion-type teaching modeled by Paul in Troas thus became impractical, not only due to the large numbers in attendance, but also because of the nominal nature of these new "disciples."[17] Furthermore, since many early church Fathers had been rhetoricians before their conversion (Tertullian, Arnobius, Cyprian, Lactantius, Augustine, etc.), it is not surprising that they would readily employ this form of communication.[18]

Follow Paul's Example

Corinth was a city full of Sophists who were masters of the persuasive art of rhetoric. They were eloquent, well respected, and had large followings.[19] It is interesting that Paul seems to have been decidedly against copying the performance-type rhetoric that was so popular in His day. Sadly, the church in Corinth had splintered into factions following various popular Christian leaders (Apollos, Peter, Paul, and even Christ). Worst yet, they had even fallen under the charm of various false, golden-tongued "super-apostles" (2Co 11:5). From his letter to the Church in Corinth, we learn that Paul spoke "not with words of

[15] Edwin Hatch, *The Influence of Greek Ideas and Usages Upon the Christian Church* (Edinburgh: Williams and Norgate, 1891), 86-115.

[16] Harold Turner, *From Temple to Meeting House* (New York: Mouton Publishers, 1979), 159-162.

[17] Hans von Campenhausen, *Ecclesiastical Authority and Spiritual Power in the Church of the First Three Centuries* (Stanford: Stanford University Press, 1969), 208.

[18] Norrington, *Preach*, 46.

[19] The Bible Effect, "1 and 2 Corinthians Historical Background", YouTube.com. Accessed August 08, 2023.

eloquent wisdom, lest the cross of Christ be emptied of its power" (1Co 1:17), and that he "did not come ... with lofty speech or wisdom" (1Co 2:1). Contrasting himself with the super apostles, Paul conceded that he was "unskilled in speaking" (2Co 11:6). Paul evidently wanted to be like the donkey that carried Jesus on Palm Sunday; the crowds hardly noticed the donkey—they looked at Jesus. They cheered Jesus, not the donkey.[20]

Reject Rhetoric

So, what's the point? Today, in a small, Roman-villa sized church, composed of genuine believers, the continued use of ancient Roman rhetoric should be seriously questioned. Don't simply copy what big churches are forced to do because of their size. Presenting messages wherein the congregation passively listens in silence is not the best way to cause learning, and is wholly inappropriate in a smaller setting.

Preaching

The word "preach" has, frankly, been overworked in our English Bibles. Over thirty different Greek words were all translated as "preach" in the King James Version, heavily influencing most subsequent English translations.[21] It would be a mistake to assume that the New Testament activity referred to as preaching is similar to that undertaken weekly by modern preachers in their pulpits.[22]

euangellizo

One common Greek word typically translated as "preach" is *eu-angellizo* (transliterated "evangelize").[23] As might be expected, it refers to evangelism. For example, Paul wrote that Christ sent him to "preach

---

[20] *Adrianism: The Collected Wit and Wisdom of Adrian Rogers* (Collierville, Innovo Publishing: 2016), 319.

[21] Norrington, *Preach*, 27.

[22] Norrington, *Preach*, 27.

[23] The noun form, *euangelion*, means "good news"—the gospel.

the gospel" (translated from a single word, *euangellizo*, 1Co 1:17). This activity happened in synagogues, markets, and places like Mars Hill. Since New Testament church meetings were designed for the edification of believers (1Co 14:26), not the evangelization of unbelievers, this type of preaching was not typical in a weekly gathering of the church. R.H. Mounce commented that as used in the New Testament, preaching "is not religious discourse to a closed group of initiates...."[24]

kérusso

Another common Greek word historically rendered as "preach" is *kérusso*. It, too, is usually associated with evangelism.[25] For example, "how are they to preach (*kérusso*) unless they are sent?" (Ro 10:15). In classical Greek, it indicated a public, authoritative announcement that demanded compliance.[26] *kérusso*, in the first century, meant "announce, make known" (historically by a herald).[27] However, we should not limit our thinking to only one method of heralding, such as the open-air gospel preaching done by Whitefield and Wesley. *kérusso* can also simply have the sense of giving notice or informing.[28] For example, if someone quietly shared the gospel with the person he was sitting next to, he has "preached" to him (without ever raising his voice). New Testament gospel heralding, however it was done, was directed primarily to the lost, not the assembled church. C.H. Dodd defined New Testament preaching as "the public proclamation of Christianity to the non-Christian world."[29]

---

[24] RH Mounce, "Preaching", *New Bible Dictionary*, 2nd edition, JD Douglas, ed., (Wheaton: Tyndale, 1982), 961.

[25] Norrington, *Preach*, 32.

[26] U. Becker, D. Muller, "Proclamation, Preach, Kerygma", *New International Dictionary of New Testament Theology*, Colin Brown, ed., Vol. 3 (Grand Rapids: Zondervan, 1978), 45.

[27] Bauer, *Lexicon*, 431.

[28] Becker, "Proclamation", 47.

[29] Mounce, "Preaching", 961.

Preach the Word

What about the few texts that seem to support preaching (*kérusso*) the Bible to Christians in church meetings? For example, Paul charged Timothy to "preach (*kérusso*) the word; be ready in season and out of season; reprove, rebuke, and exhort, with complete patience and teaching" (2Ti 4:2). Paul's reference to the "word" (*logos*) likely refers to the Scriptures referenced two verses earlier in 3:16 ("All Scripture is breathed out by God"). It is noteworthy that Paul's command to "preach the word" was to be characterized by "complete patience and <u>teaching</u>" (4:2). As previously stated, *kérusso* fundamentally means to "make known." Part of the way in which Timothy was charged to make known the Word of God was clearly through "teaching." There are many ways to make the Scriptures known besides the modern concept of preaching a sermon.

katangello

A less common word that could be translated as "preach" is *katangello*. However, in the New Testament it does not refer to any particular form of proclamation.[30] How these proclamations were carried out has been lost to history. To envision *katangello* to be the same as a preacher preaching a sermon would be to assume too much. My goal is not to prove that there never were lectures in early church meetings, but rather that there was another way that was more common and more effective—dialogue teaching.

Are all preachers?

With all the emphasis today on the "centrality of preaching,"[31] it is worth noting that in 1 Corinthians 11-14—a lengthy section on ecclesiology—neither preachers nor preaching are ever mentioned. In this section, when emphasizing the great diversity of spiritual gifts given to build up the church, Paul did not ask, "Are all preachers?" Instead, he asked,

---

[30] Becker, "Proclamation", 45.

[31] "Mohler cites preaching's centrality in 'Power in the Pulpit' seminar", BaptistPress.org.

"Are all teachers?" (1Co 12:29). The Romans 12 directory of spiritual gifts lists "teaching" (*didaskalia*), but not preaching (*kérusso*, 12:7).

Prophets = Preachers?

Some have speculated that the prophets referenced in 1 Corinthians 14 were the equivalent to modern preachers. Let's assume that it is the case. The text makes it obvious that on any given Lord's Day, two or three preached (not only one as is common today). Furthermore, the preacher could be interrupted and stopped mid-sermon: "If a revelation is made to another sitting there, let the first be silent" (14:30). Even more interesting, each sermon was to be judged right there, on the spot: "let two or three prophets speak, and let the others pass judgment" (14:29, NASV). That would certainly make for an interesting church meeting! However, Thomas Schreiner has pointed out that the prophets were not like modern preachers. Prophets, unlike preachers, did not exposit Scripture based on their own prior careful study. Rather, they spoke spontaneously when they got messages directly from God (1Co 14:29-30).[32]

Labor in the Word and Doctrine

1 Timothy 5:17 refers to elders who were involved with both "preaching and teaching" (ESV). The Greek underneath "preach" is *logos*, which fundamentally simply refers to a literal "word" uttered when talking.[33] It could also refer to a speech, but is not the typical Greek word used for what we consider today to be preaching (*kérusso*). And, whatever its meaning, it is clearly different from the teaching (*didaskalia*) mentioned in the same text. Since *logos* can also refer to God's written Word,[34] Scripture may be what Paul had in mind, not preaching. That is, church leaders who labor hard studying the Scriptures and

---

[32] Thomas Schreiner, *Spiritual Gifts: What They Are & Why They Matter* (Nashville: B&H Publishing, 2018), chapter 6.

[33] Bauer, *Lexicon*, 477.

[34] Bauer, *Lexicon*, 478.

subsequently in teaching them are worthy of double honor. Thus, the KJV has: "… they who labour in the <u>word</u> and doctrine." Again, the point is not that preaching a sermon absolutely never could have occurred in a church meeting. The point is that unlike teaching, preaching a sermon was not a regular weekly occurrence.

Prescription

We should evaluate the opportunity cost of the weekly preaching of sermons in smaller churches. The communication styles we see in the New Testament were simply not the same as a Western-styled pulpit ministry. Though much good comes from preaching, discussion-type teaching is more effective, and arguably more biblical.

Challenging Questions

How can we as church leaders best serve the Church in the way we teach so as to most effectively make disciples? Custom has been described as the fiercest tyrant of them all. Let us not unwittingly be like those Jesus confronted who set aside the Word of God for the sake of their tradition. It is far better to follow the New Testament example, and stop lecturing in smaller churches. Ask challenging questions that will cause people to think and to discover truth for themselves. Adopt the discussion-style teaching modeled by both Jesus and Paul.

"Go therefore and make disciples of all nations, baptizing them in the name of the Father and of the Son and of the Holy Spirit, <u>teaching</u> them to observe all that I have commanded you."[35]

NTRF.org has audio, video, articles, and a teacher's discussion guide on participatory church meetings.

---

[35] Matthew 28:19-20

Strategy #3

Fellowship in the Breaking of Bread

Every believer has a dinner reservation at the Wedding Banquet of the Lamb. Jesus also has dinner plans for you this coming Lord's Day! The Lord's Supper was originally celebrated every week, *as an actual meal*. This fellowship in the breaking of bread is the ideal setting for building the close relationships that form a basis for personalized disciple making. It also creates supernatural unity, fantastic fellowship, and personal holiness in view of His return. *Has the Lord's supper, in your church, become a lost supper?*

Profit

The bread and cup look back to Jesus' death on the cross to pay for sin. The meal adds a forward look. When celebrated as a meal in a joyful, wedding atmosphere, the Lord's Supper typifies the wedding supper of the Lamb. It is a regular reminder of Jesus' promise to return and eat it with us, and everyone who hopes in His appearing purifies himself, just as He is pure.

Another major benefit is the fellowship and encouragement that is experienced by each member of Christ's body. The leadership gets to enjoy the fellowship along with everyone else. This relaxed, unhurried fellowship meal with God's family is a significant means of edifying the Church, building community, cementing ties of love, and creating supernatural unity. It is the perfect setting to "stir one another up to love and good works ... encouraging one another" (Heb 10:24-25). The strong relationships formed through this holy meal also create a firm foundation for effective and personalized disciple making.

Professors

Scholarly opinion is clearly weighted toward the conclusion that the Lord's Supper was originally eaten as a meal. In *New Testament Theology*, Donald Guthrie stated that the apostle Paul "sets the Lord's supper in the context of the fellowship meal."[1]

Editor of the notable Evangelical commentary series *New International Commentary on the New Testament*, Gordon Fee, noted "the nearly universal phenomenon of cultic meals as a part of worship in antiquity." He asserted that "in the early church the Lord's Supper was most likely eaten as, or in conjunction with, such a meal." Fee further noted: "From the beginning, the *Last* Supper was for Christians not an annual Christian Passover, but a regularly repeated meal in 'honor of the Lord,' hence the *Lord's* Supper."[2]

In the *New Bible Dictionary*, G.W. Grogan observed: "The administration of the Eucharist shows it set in the context of a fellowship supper.... The separation of the meal or Agape from the Eucharist lies outside the times of the NT."[3] In his commentary on 1 Corinthians,

---

[1]   Donald Guthrie, *New Testament Theology* (Downers Grove: Inter-Varsity, 1981), 758.

[2]   Fee, "Corinthians," 532, 555.

[3]   G. W. Grogan, "Love Feast," *The New Bible Dictionary*, ed. J. D. Douglas (Wheaton: Tyndale, 1982), 712.

C.K. Barrett stated: "The Lord's Supper was still at Corinth an ordinary meal to which acts of symbolical significance were attached, rather than a purely symbolical meal."[4]

United Methodist Publishing House editor John Gooch wrote: "In the first century, the Lord's Supper included not only the bread and the cup but an entire meal."[5] Yale professor J.J. Pelikan concluded: "Often, if not always, it was celebrated in the setting of a common meal."[6]

Proof

The Passover Feast

The setting for the first Lord's Supper was the Passover *Feast*. Jesus and His disciples reclined around a table heaping with food (Ex 12, Dt 16). Jesus took bread and compared it to His body "*while* they were eating" (Mt 26:26; emphasis mine). "*After* the supper" (Lk 22:20; emphasis mine), Jesus took the cup and compared it to His blood, soon to be poured out for sin. Timing is everything. The bread and wine of the Lord's Supper were introduced in the context of an actual meal. The twelve would have naturally understood the Lord's Supper to be a meal also. The Greek word for "supper" (*deipnon*) refers to the main meal toward evening.[7] It is frequently translated as banquet. Arguably, it never refers to anything less than a full meal.

Eschatological Eating

At the Last Supper, Jesus said: "I confer on you a kingdom ... so that you may eat and drink at my table in my kingdom" (Lk 22:29–30). What is the reason for this eschatological eating? First-century Jews thought of heaven as a time of feasting at the Messiah's table. For example, a

4　C. K. Barrett, "The First Epistle to the Corinthians," *Black's New Testament Commentary* (Peabody, MA: Hendrickson, 1968), 276.

5　John Gooch, *Christian History & Biography*, Issue 37 (Carol Stream, IL: Christianity Today, 1993), 3.

6　Jaroslav Pelikan, "Eucharist," *Encyclopaedia Britannica*, ed. Warren Preece, Vol. 8 (Chicago: William Benton, Publisher, 1973), 808.

7　Bauer, *Lexicon*, 173. Used in 1 Corinthians 11:20.

Jewish leader once said to Jesus: "Blessed is everyone who will eat bread in the kingdom of God!" (Lk 14:15). Jesus Himself spoke of those who will "take their places at the feast with Abraham, Isaac and Jacob in the kingdom of heaven" (Mt 8:11).[8] Celebrating the Lord's Supper as a meal is typifies the Wedding Banquet of the Lamb—heaven on earth!

A Feast of Rich Food

Isaiah described the coming Messianic feast in this way: "the LORD of hosts will make for all peoples a feast of rich food, a feast of well-aged wine, of rich food full of marrow, of aged wine well refined … He will swallow up death forever; and the Lord GOD will wipe away tears from all faces, and the reproach of his people he will take away from all the earth, for the LORD has spoken" (Isa 25:6–8). The Book of Revelation describes a future time of feasting at the Lamb's wedding banquet (Rev 19:9).

The Wedding Banquet of the Lamb

When the early church observed the Lord's Supper, which included the bread and the cup, it clearly was as a true meal. It is important to appreciate why the Lord's Supper was originally a meal. It is an image and foretaste of what we will be doing when Jesus returns to eat it with us. *What better way to typify the marriage banquet of the Lamb than a meal manifesting all the excitement, fellowship, and love of the heavenly feast?*

One Goes Hungry

The most extensive treatment of the Lord's Supper is found in 1 Corinthians 10–11. The church in Corinth clearly celebrated it as a meal. Sadly, class and cultural divisions resulted in their communion meals doing more harm than good (11:17–18). The upper class, not

---

[8]   This picture of heaven as eating in God's presence may have originated from the Sinai experience. When the elders went with Moses to the top of the mountain, God did not raise his hand against them. Instead, "they saw God, and they ate and drank" (Ex 24:11).

wanting to dine with those of a lower social class, evidently came to the gathering early to avoid the poor. By the time the working-class believers arrived, delayed perhaps by employment constraints, all the food had been eaten. The poor went home hungry (11:21–22). The wealthy failed to esteem their impoverished brethren as equal members of the body of Christ (11:23–32).

His Own Meal

The Corinthian abuse was so serious that the *Lord's* Supper had instead become their *own* suppers: "When you come together, it is not the Lord's supper that you eat. For in eating, each one goes ahead with his own meal," 11:20–21 (supper and meal are from the same Greek word). If merely eating one's own supper had been the entire objective, then private dining at home would have sufficed. Thus, Paul asked the rich: "Do you not have houses to eat and drink in?" (11:22). Considering the nature of the abuse, it is evident that the Corinthian church regularly partook of the Lord's Supper as a meal.

Instituted by the Apostles

It has been suggested that the abuses in Corinth led Paul to end the meal. For example, the original commentary in the 1599 *Geneva Bible* stated: "The Apostle thinketh it good to take away the love feasts, for their abuse, although they had been a long time, and with commendation used in Churches, and were appointed and instituted by the Apostles."[9] This prompts the following question: Would Paul have single-handedly overturned a practice that had been established by Jesus, taught by the apostles, and upheld by all the churches? We think not. However, the *Geneva Bible*'s commentary affirms the simultaneous celebration of the Lord's Supper and the love feast, as instituted by the apostles.

---

9   *1599 Geneva Bible* (White Hall: Tolle Lege Press, 2006), 1180.

Wait for Each Other

It has been said that the best antidote to abuse is not disuse, but appropriate use. Paul's solution to Corinthian abuse was *not* to do away with the meal. Instead, Paul wrote: "when you come together to eat, wait for each other" (11:33). Only those who are so famished that they could not wait for the others were instructed to "eat at home" (11:34). Acclaimed commentator C.K. Barrett cautioned: "Paul's point is that, if the rich wish to eat and drink on their own, enjoying better food than their poorer brothers, they should do this at home; if they cannot wait for others (verse 33), if they must indulge to excess, they can at least keep the church's common meal free from practices that can only bring discredit upon it.... Paul simply means that those who are so hungry that they cannot wait for their brothers should satisfy their hunger before they leave home, in order that decency and order may prevail in the assembly."[10]

Section Summary

In summary, it is clear from Scripture that in the early church, the bread and wine of the Lord's Supper were eaten in the context of a meal. Communion was celebrated not only with the Lord through the elements but also with other believers through the meal. This early church practice builds community and unity, edifies the church, and typifies the coming eschatological feast. Celebrating the Lord's Supper as a meal is like participating in the rehearsal dinner for a great wedding and feast.

Perspective: A Future Focus

Fritz Reinecker stated: "The Passover celebrated two events, the deliverance from Egypt and the anticipated coming Messianic deliverance."[11]

---

[10]   Barrett, "Corinthians," 263 & 277.

[11]   Fritz Reinecker and Cleon Rogers, *Linguistic Key to the Greek New Testament* (Grand Rapids: Zondervan, 1980), 207.

It looked both to the past and the future. When Jesus transformed the Passover Feast into the Lord's Supper, He endowed it both past and future characteristics. It looks back to Jesus' sacrifice as the ultimate Passover Lamb who delivers His people from their sins, and it looks forward to the time when He will come again and eat it with us. For example, the *Baptist Faith and Message 2000* states: "The Lord's Supper is a symbolic act of obedience whereby members of the church, through partaking of the bread and the fruit of the vine, memorialize the death of the Redeemer and *anticipate His second coming*" (emphasis added).[12]

Eschatological Overtones

R.P. Martin, professor of New Testament at Fuller Theological Seminary, wrote of the "eschatological overtones" in the Lord's Supper "with a forward look to the advent in glory."[13] The future kingdom of God weighed on the Lord's mind during the Last Supper. Jesus first mentioned the future at the beginning of the Passover: "I will not eat it until it is fulfilled in the kingdom of God" (Lk 22:16). "Until," *heos hutou*, is forward-looking. It indicates a future occurrence. Furthermore, Jesus' use of "fulfilled" suggests that there is something prophetic about the Lord's Supper.

Not Until the Kingdom Comes

It is often overlooked that Jesus mentioned the future while passing the cup: "from now on I will not drink of the fruit of the vine until the kingdom of God comes" (Lk 22:18). Every time we partake of the cup, Jesus' promise to return to drink it with us should be considered. After the supper, He referred to the future meal yet again: "I confer on you a kingdom ... so that you may eat and drink at my table in my kingdom" (Lk 22:29–30).

---

12 "The Baptist Faith and Message," sbc.net, accessed September 6, 2016.
13 R. P. Martin, "The Lord's Supper," *The New Bible Dictionary*, ed. J. D. Douglas (Wheaton: Tyndale, 1982), 709.

The Heavenly Banquet to Come

Thus, we see that Jesus imbued the Lord's Supper with several forward-looking characteristics. As an actual meal, it prefigures the marriage supper of the Lamb. When we partake of the cup, we should be reminded of Jesus' promise: "I will not drink of the fruit of the vine until the kingdom of God comes" (Lk 22:18). The following description is provided in the *Encyclopaedia Britannica*: "Early Christianity regarded this institution as a mandate ... learning to know, even in this present life, the joy of the heavenly banquet that was to come in the kingdom of God ... the past, the present, and the future came together in the Eucharist."[14]

Until He Comes

1 Corinthians 11:26 reveals that through the Lord's Supper, we proclaim the Lord's death "until" He comes. The word "until" normally denotes a time frame. For example, an umbrella is used *until* it stops raining; then it is put away. Using the umbrella does not cause the rain to stop. However, Paul's statement focuses on the reason for proclaiming the Lord's death. The Greek word for "until," *achri hou*, is unusual. Conservative German theology professor Fritz Rienecker indicated that this usage (with an aorist subjunctive verb) denotes much more than a mere time frame. It can denote a goal or an objective.[15]

The Goal Is His Return

In *The Eucharistic Words of Jesus*, argument was made that the Greek words *achri hou*, which underlies "until" (1Co 11:26), are not simply a temporal reference. It functions as a final clause. In other words, the meal functions as a constant reminder to God to bring about

---

[14] Pelikan, "Eucharist," 808.
[15] Reinecker, *Linguistic*, 427. Other instances of this construction in eschatological passages include Luke 21:24, Romans 11:25, and 1 Corinthians 15:25.

the Second Coming.[16] Paul instructed the church to partake of the bread and cup as a means of proclaiming the Lord's death with the goal of His return. Thus, in proclaiming His death through the loaf and cup, the Supper anticipates His return. Dutch theologian Herman Ridderbos stated: "It is not merely a subjective recalling to mind, but an active manifestation of the continuing and actual significance of the death of Christ. "Proclaim" in this respect has a prophetic, declaratory significance…. Everything is directed not only toward the past, but also toward the future. It is the proclamation that in the death of Christ the new and eternal covenant of grace has taken effect, if still in a provisional and not yet consummated sense."[17]

Maranatha!

It is interesting that the earliest believers used *maranatha* ("Our Lord, come") in the *Didache* as a prayer in relation to the Lord's Supper, "a context at once eucharistic and eschatological."[18] Linking this to the situation in Corinth, R. P. Martin wrote: "*Maranatha* in 1 Cor. 16:22 may very well be placed in a Eucharistic setting so that the conclusion of the letter ends with the invocation 'Our Lord, come!' and prepares the scene for the celebration of the meal after the letter has been read to the congregation."[19]

Purpose # 1: Community
Food & Fellowship

In ancient Jewish culture, sharing a meal symbolized acceptance and fellowship. Thus, in Revelation 3:20, Jesus offered to "eat" (*deipneo*) with anyone who heard His voice and opened the door. One of the major blessings of celebrating the Lord's Supper as a meal is the genuine

---

[16]   Joachim Jeremias, *The Eucharistic Words of Jesus* (New York: Charles Scribner's Sons, 1966), 252–254.

[17]   Herman Ridderbos, *Paul: An Outline of His Theology*, trans. John R. deWitt (Grand Rapids: Eerdmans, 1975), 422.

[18]   Barrett, "Corinthians," 397.

[19]   Martin, "Supper," 709.

fellowship that everyone enjoys. This theme of fellowship in feasting is evident in the book of Acts. A casual reading of Acts 2:42 suggests that the Church had four priorities: the teachings of the apostles, fellowship, the breaking of bread, and prayer. However, a closer examination reveals that the focus was on only three activities: teaching, fellowship in the breaking of bread, and prayer. (In Greek, "fellowship" and "breaking of bread" are simultaneous activities.)[20]

The Breaking of Bread = The Lord's Supper

It was F.F. Bruce's position that the fellowship described in Acts 2:42 was manifested in the breaking of bread.[21] The Lord's Supper has often been associated with the phrase "breaking of bread," which appears throughout the book of Acts. For example, Bruce argued that "breaking of bread" denotes "something more than the ordinary partaking of food together: the regular observance of the Lord's Supper is no doubt indicated ... this observance appears to have formed part of an ordinary meal."[22] The early church enjoyed the Lord's Supper as a time of fellowship and gladness as would have been the case at a wedding banquet: "breaking bread in their homes, they received their food with glad and generous hearts, praising God and having favor with all the people" (Acts 2:46–47). The Lord's Supper was characterized as a time of fellowship. *Sounds inviting, doesn't it?*

The Lord's Funeral?

Many churches observe the Lord's Supper in a funereal atmosphere. An organ plays reflective music softly. Every head is bowed, and every eye is closed as the members of the congregation quietly search

---

[20] In most English versions, "and" is placed between "teaching" and "fellowship" then again between "bread" and "prayer," but not between "fellowship" and "bread" (Acts 2:42). The reason is that in some Greek manuscripts, the words "fellowship" and "breaking of bread" are connected as simultaneous activities (no kai between fellowship and the breaking of bread).

[21] F. F. Bruce, "The Book of Acts," *New International Commentary on the New Testament* (Grand Rapids: Eerdmans, 1981), 79.

[22] Ibid., 79.

their souls for sins that need to be confessed. In an arrangement that is eerily reminiscent of a casket, the elements are laid out on a narrow rectangular table that is covered with a white cloth at the front of the church. Pallbearer-like deacons solemnly distribute the elements. Dutch theologian Karl Deddens noted: "Under the influence of pietism and mysticism, a sense of 'unworthiness' is awakened within them, and they become afraid that they may be 'eating and drinking judgment unto themselves.' As for those who were still bold enough to go to the table of the Lord, their faces suggest that a funeral is under way rather than a celebration."[23] *Is this somber approach to the Supper in keeping with the apostles' tradition?*

Unworthy Manner

It was the unworthy *manner*, not unworthy *people*, that Paul criticized (1Co 11:27). He was referring to drunkenness at the Lord's Table, conniving to avoid eating with the poor, and humiliating the poor subsequent had to go home hungry. This failure of the rich to recognize the body of the Lord in their poorer brethren resulted in divine judgment. Many of them were sick, and a number had even died (1Co 11:27–32). Indeed, every person ought to examine himself to be sure he is not guilty of the same gross sin: failing to recognize the body of the Lord in the other believers (1Co 11:28–29). Once we each have evaluated ourselves, we can come to the meal without fear of judgment to enjoy the fellowship of the Lord's Supper as the true wedding banquet it is intended to be.

Neighborhood Bar

We all desire church relationships that are genuine and meaningful: not just a friendly church but one where our friends are. The Lord's Supper can help to make this a reality. A middle-aged man, new in

---

[23] Karl Deddens, *Where Everything Points to Him*, trans. Theodore Plantinga (Neerlandia: Inheritance Publications, 1993), 93.

Christ and to the church, sat through several traditional Sunday services. Finally, he asked: "I see people greet each other just before the service. As soon as it ends, they hug good-bye and quickly head home. I'm not getting to know anyone. What is the Christian equivalent of the neighborhood bar?"[24] Celebrating the Lord's Supper weekly as a relaxed fellowship meal is the biblical answer to his question.

The Central Rite of Worship

The holy meal should be celebrated often to maximize the fellowship aspect. For the early believers, participation in the Lord's Supper was one of the main reasons for their coming together as a church every Lord's Day. *Encyclopaedia Britannica* has described the Lord's Supper as "the central rite of Christian worship" and "an indispensable component of the Christian service since the earliest days of the church."[25]

The Lord's Day & The Lord's Supper

The first evidence of weekly communion is grammatical. To Christians, Sunday is the "Lord's Day" (Rev 1:10), the day Jesus rose from the dead. This is a translation of *kuriakon hemeran*, unique technical Greek wording. It is literally "the day belonging to the Lord." The phrase "belonging to the Lord" is from *kuriakos*, which is found in the New Testament in only Revelation 1:10 and 1 Corinthians 11:20, where it refers to the Supper as "belonging to the Lord" (*kuriakon deipnon*). The connection between these two unusual but identical ways in which these words are used must not be overlooked. The *supper* belonging to the Lord was eaten every week on the *day* belonging to the Lord. The Lord's Day and the Lord's Supper are a weekly package deal.[26]

---

24 Conversation with the author, mid–1980s.
25 Pelikan, "Eucharist," 807.
26 Eric Svendsen, *The Table of the Lord* (Atlanta: NTRF, 1997), 140.

We Came Together to Break Bread

More evidence for the weekly celebration of the Lord's Supper is found in the only clear reason given in Scripture for regular church meetings: to eat the Lord's Supper. In Acts 20:7, Luke stated: "On the first day of the week we came together to break bread." The words "to break bread" are a telic infinitive, denoting a purpose or an objective. They met for the purpose of breaking bread (the Lord's Supper).

When You Come Together

Another New Testament passage in which the purpose of a church gathering is stated is 1 Corinthians 11:17–22. The "meetings" (11:17) were doing more harm than good because when they came "together as a church" (11:18a), there were deep divisions. Thus, Paul wrote: "when you come together, it is not the Lord's Supper you eat" (11:20). Thus, the ostensible reason for the weekly church meetings was to eat the Lord's Supper.

Come Together to Eat

The third and last reference to the explicitly stated reason for assembly is found in 1 Corinthians 11:33, "When you come together *to eat*, wait for each other" (italics mine). As before, the verse indicates that they came together to eat. The Scriptures give no other reason for weekly church meetings. It is clear that there were times for prayer, praise, and teaching each Sunday; however, the central focus was communion.

Early Testimony

Early extra-biblical sources also indicate that the church originally celebrated the Lord's Supper weekly, such as Justin Martyr's *First Apology*, written in the middle of the second century. Another example is the *Didache*. Around A.D. 200, Hippolytus wrote of the typical church meeting in Rome—it included the Lord's Supper.

Christ's Command

It has been generalized that Protestant churches replaced the altar with the pulpit. Never-the-less, John Calvin advocated weekly communion.[27] Karl Deddens wrote: "If the Lord's Supper were celebrated more often, we should not view such a change as an accommodation to 'sacramentalists' who wish to place less emphasis on the service of the Word; rather, we should view it as an execution of Christ's command...."[28] The fellowship and encouragement that each member enjoys in such a weekly gathering is significant. This aspect of the Church's Sunday meeting should not be rushed or replaced. It is also important that the meeting be devoted to prayer and the apostle's teachings (Acts 2:42); however, this should not be at the expense of the weekly Lord's Supper. The weekly celebration of the Holy Meal adds an unparalleled dynamic to church meetings.

Purpose #2: Supernatural Unity

One Cup, One Loaf

The celebration of the Lord's Supper each week as a fellowship meal makes a significant contribution to unity. Also important is the visual presentation of the elements. The Scriptures refer to the cup of thanksgiving (a single cup, 1Co 10:16) and one loaf: "Because there is one loaf, we, who are many, are one body, for we all partake of the one loaf" (1Co 10:17).[29] If using one cup and one loaf symbolizes our oneness in Christ, then using pre-broken crackers and multiple tiny cups represents disunity, division, and individualism.

Supernatural Unity

The single loaf not only symbolizes our unity in Christ, but

---

[27] David Koyzis, "The Lord's Supper: How Often?" ReformedWorship.org, accessed September 1, 2016.

[28] Deddens, "Everything Points," 93.

[29] NIV.

according to 1 Corinthians 10:17, partaking of it actually *creates unity*. The words of the inspired text should be noted: "Because" there is one loaf, therefore we are one body, "for" we all partake of the one loaf (1Co 10:17). One scholar argued that the Lord's Supper was "intended as a means of fostering the unity of the church...."[30] Professor Gerd Theissen said: "Because all have eaten portions of the same element, they have become a unity in which they have come as close to one another as members of the same body, as if the bodily boundaries between and among people had been transcended."[31] In their commentary on Corinthians, Archibald Robertson and Alfred Plummer concluded: "The single loaf is a symbol and an instrument of unity."[32] Gordon Fee wrote of the "solidarity of the fellowship of believers created by their all sharing 'the one loaf.'"[33]

Wait for Each Other

Some in Corinth were guilty of partaking of the Lord's Supper unworthily (1Co 11:27). Shameful class divisions cut at the heart of the unity that the Lord's Supper is designed to symbolize. What was Paul's solution to the harmful meetings? "So then, my brothers, when you come together to eat, wait for each other" (1Co 11:33). A partial reason for the Corinthians' lack of unity was their failure to eat the Lord's Supper together as a meal centered around the one cup and one loaf.

That They May Be One

Jesus prayed "that they may be one even as we are one" (Jn 17:11). In the Lord's Supper, we express our oneness in Christ. The Lord's Supper is a fundamental practice that reflects the eternal image of the

---

30 Pelikan, "Eucharist," 807.

31 Gerd Theissen, *The Social Setting of Pauline Christianity: Essays on Corinth* (Eugene: Wipf & Stock Publishers, 1982), 165.

32 Archibald Robertson & Alfred Plummer, "1 Corinthians," *The International Critical Commentary on the Holy Scriptures of the Old and New Testaments* (New York: Charles Scribner's Sons, 1911), 213.

33 Fee, "Corinthians," 515.

Church and Christianity: "There is one body and one Spirit—just as you were called to the one hope that belongs to your call—one Lord, one faith, one baptism, one God and Father of all, who is over all and through all and in all" (Eph 4:4–6). Our unity in Christ is a powerful witness. Jesus prayed that we "may all be one … so that the world may believe that you have sent me" (Jn 17:21).

Purpose #3: Jesus' Return
God Remembers Covenant Promises

In the covenant God made with Noah, He promised to never again destroy the earth by flood. With respect to the rainbow, God declared: "Whenever the rainbow appears in the clouds, I will see it and *remember* the everlasting covenant between God and all living creatures" (Gn 9:16; emphasis added). Wayne Grudem noted that the Bible "frequently speaks of God 'remembering' something and therefore I do not think it inappropriate or inconsistent for us to speak this way when we want to refer to God's awareness of events that have happened in our past, events he recognizes as already having occurred and therefore as being 'past.'"[34] It is biblical to say that God remembers covenant promises.

Abraham & Sinai Remembered

In His covenant with Abraham, God promised to bring the Israelites out of Egyptian bondage. Accordingly, at the appointed time, "God heard their groaning, and *God remembered* his covenant with Abraham" (Ex 2:24; emphasis added). During the Babylonian captivity, God made a promise to the Jews: "*I will remember* my covenant with you" (the Sinai covenant, Eze 16:60; emphasis added). God remembers covenant promises.

---

[34] Wayne Grudem, "The Nature of Divine Eternity, A Response to William Craig," Wayne-Grudem.com, accessed September 03, 2016.

The New Covenant Reminder

In the Lord's Supper, the fruit of the vine represents the "blood of the covenant" (Mt 26:28), and the bread symbolizes Jesus' body. Jesus said to partake of the bread "in remembrance of me" (Lk 22:19). The bread and wine are reminders of His body and blood given for us. The Greek word for "remembrance" (*anamnesis*) fundamentally means "reminder." A reminder can be a prompt about either a previous or future occurrence. Translating *ananmesis* as "remembrance" leads to the exclusive focus on Jesus' past sacrifice on the cross. However, if *anamnesis* is translated as "reminder," it could be understood to refer to both the past (Jesus' death on the cross) and the future (Jesus' promise to return).

It Belongs to Jesus

As we have already seen, God remembers covenant promises. Another very significant function of the Lord's Supper is as a reminder to Jesus Himself of His new covenant promise to return.[35] Jesus said: "Do this unto my reminder." The word "my" in "my reminder" is a translation of the Greek *emou*. More than a mere personal pronoun, it is a possessive pronoun. This suggests that the reminder is not simply about Jesus; it actually belongs to Jesus. It is *His* reminder. Theologian Joachim Jeremias understood Jesus to use *anamnesis* in the sense of a reminder for God: "The Lord's Supper would thus be an enacted prayer."[36] Just as seeing the rainbow reminds God of His covenant never to flood the world again, so too Jesus' seeing us partake of the Lord's Supper reminds Him of His promise to return to eat it with us. Thus, it is designed to be a prayer to ask Jesus to return ("Thy kingdom come," Lk 11:2). God remembers covenant promises.

---

[35] Statements about God's remembering or being reminded are anthropomorphic. An omniscient God neither forgets nor needs to be reminded.

[36] K.H. Bartels, "Remember," *New International Dictionary of New Testament Theology*, Vol. III, ed. Colin Brown (Grand Rapids: Zondervan, 1981), 244–245.

Section Summary

In summary, when we partake of the bread and wine, we are re-minded of Jesus' body and blood, which were given for the remission of sin. Along with Jesus, we should be reminded of His promise to return to eat it with us. The celebration of the Lord's Supper is an enacted prayer that reminds Jesus to return. This weekly reminder of the im-minence of our Lord's return can be a motivation for holy living: "we know that when he appears we will be like him, because we shall see him as he is. And everyone who thus hopes in him purifies himself as he is pure" (1Jn 3:2–3). *Maranatha!*

Proposition

A Feast Turned Famine

As was demonstrated above, there is general agreement within scholarly circles that the early church celebrated the Lord's Supper as a genuine meal. However, the post-apostolic church has had little use for this practice. The transition from genuine meal to token ritual was gradual, taking place during the mid-second century in some places to mid-third century in others: "The key to transition was connected to the size of the congregation. The larger ones transitioned earlier. They needed a more efficient way to gather people and distribute the most significant symbols of the meal.... The smaller congregations continued to use meals until the mid-third century when the standard practice became the more recognizable Eucharist officiated by key leaders such as bishops and their approved leaders.... Researchers have difficulty precisely understanding why this transition took place. By the fourth century, it is clear the tradition of full meals held in homes is gone. The Eucharistic rite inside of a basilica or other large church becomes the new norm."[37]

In his role as bishop, Eusebius consecrated a church building in

---

[37] Greg Mamula, "Early Christian Table Fellowship Becomes Eucharistic Rite," unpublished paper, 2015, 16–18.

Tyre. At the dedication, Eusebius spoke of the most holy altar as the center of the building. The Synod of Laodicea later forbade the celebration of the Lord's Supper in private homes (late 300s). Peter Davids and Siegfried Grossman offered this comment: "Once you have an altar with 'holy food,' mixing it with the common food of a communal meal appears profane. Thus, the focus on the table as altar brings about the forbidding of celebrating the Lord's Supper in houses. The irony is that in the tabernacle and temple the central act of worship was a family meal in the presence of the deity, the temple being part slaughterhouse and part bar-b-que, as well as being the place where animal fat was burned and incense was offered."[38]

A Missed Blessing

Throughout history, the church has sometimes deviated from New Testament patterns. For example, for more than a millennium, credo-only baptism was essentially unheard of in Christendom. However, since the Reformation, this long-neglected apostolic tradition has been widely practiced. Another example is the separation of church and state, a New Testament example that was disregarded during the long period in Europe when church and state were merged. Today, however, most believers appreciate this separation. The church today might be missing out on a great blessing in its neglect of the early church's practice surrounding the Lord's Supper. *Celebrating the Lord's Supper weekly as a meal was the practice of the early church; should we not follow this example?*

Prescription

A Commendable Tradition

For many church leaders, the New Testament example of the Lord's Supper as a weekly fellowship meal is a precious historical memory that

---

[38] Peter Davids & Siegfried Grossmann, "The Church in the House," paper, 1982.

they feel no compulsion to follow. However, Scripture indicates that the practices of the early church should serve as more than a historical academic record. For example, 1 Corinthians 11–14 concerns church practice. The passage begins with praise for the Corinthian church for following Paul's *traditions*: "I commend you because you remember me in everything and maintain the traditions even as I delivered them to you" (11:2). *Paradosis*, the Greek word for tradition, means "that which is passed on."[39] This same Greek word is used as a verb form in 1 Corinthians 11:23 with regard to the practice of the Lord's Supper (that it was passed on from Jesus to Paul and then to the Corinthians). *Do we really want to disregard a Lord's Supper tradition that was handed down by Jesus Himself?*

An Imperative

It is often mistakenly thought that there are no directions to follow tradition. However, 2 Thessalonians 2:15 specifically commands: "stand firm and hold to the traditions."[40] Thus, we should adhere to not just apostolic *teachings* but also apostolic *traditions*.[41] The context of 2 Thessalonians 2:15 is the apostles' tradition about the end times. The word "traditions" (2:15) is plural. The author was including traditions besides about the second coming. *Should it not also apply to his traditions regarding church order, as indicated in the New Testament?* [42]

Section Summary

The Lord's Supper was the primary purpose the early church gathered each Lord's Day. It was celebrated as a feast in a joyful wedding

---

[39] Rienecker, *Linguistic*, 423.

[40] Imperative mode in Greek.

[41] Apostolic traditions, as recorded in the New Testament, are to be distinguished from later Catholic and Orthodox traditions.

[42] A similar attitude toward tradition is expressed in 2 Thessalonians 3:6–7a. Tradition here refers to practice rather than just doctrine. The apostles clearly wanted the churches to follow their traditions of *both* theology and practice. Should we limit those apostolic traditions that we follow to eschatology and work habits?

atmosphere rather than a somber funereal atmosphere. A major benefit of the Supper as a meal is the fellowship and encouragement each member experiences. This is the perfect setting for each member to be a minister, stirring up one another to love and good deeds. Eaten as a meal, the Supper typifies the marriage supper of the Lamb and looks to the future, which encourages holiness. There should be one cup and one loaf to both symbolize and create unity in a body of believers. The bread and wine represent Jesus' body and blood, the sign of the new covenant. They also serve as reminders of His promise to return to eat it with us. (Amen. Come quickly, Lord Jesus!)

Practicum

The Elements

One cup and one loaf, symbolic of our unity in Christ, should be visible to the congregation. Pre-broken crackers and pre-poured tiny cups represent division and individualism. The entire congregation should partake of the same cup and loaf. Anglicans have done this for centuries without obvious harm to their health.[43] Another option is to pour the wine from a large decanter (visible to all) into smaller cups, or to have each person dip his bread in the common cup.

Starting Out

Church planters can easily make the weekly celebration of the Holy Meal an integral part of the Sunday meetings from a church's inception. Existing churches might consider gradually phasing in the Lord's Supper as a meal. One approach could be to make the meal optional initially. The elements could be served as usual, followed by a meal in the fellowship hall for those who wish to participate. Members of the congregation should be given time to grow excited and tell others. Furthermore, unless they are persuaded of the Scriptural basis for the

---

[43] The alcohol in wine kills the germs.

weekly celebration of the Lord's Supper as a fellowship meal, there will be resistance over going to the trouble of preparing food to share. It is important that everyone understand the holy nature of the meal. It is not an inconvenient lunch. It is a sacred covenant meal before the Lord and with His children.

Wednesday Night Suppers

Many churches offer Wednesday night fellowship meals. The introduction of the Lord's Supper as a meal in conjunction with the existing Wednesday-night meal is a creative option but should be only a transitional step. Two thousand years of Western Christianity have rightly ingrained in believers the notion that what happens on Sundays is what is really important. The Lord's Supper, *Agapé*, was the main reason that the early church gathered each Lord's Day. Thus, the goal should be to celebrate it on Sundays in order for it to have the same prominence accorded by the apostles. Grace unto unity comes when the entire congregation, not just the minority who attend on Wednesday night, partakes of the cup and loaf. The entire congregation needs to experience the weekly fellowship of the *Agapé*.

Integration

The bread and wine were given in the context of a dinner. To avoid the impression that the Lord's Supper is the cup and loaf and everything else is merely a meal, care should be taken not to separate the elements from the meal. The food should be ready before the elements are presented so the meal can be eaten immediately afterwards. One approach is to call attention to the significance of the elements and lead in prayer. Then, the head of each household should come forward to take the elements back to his family. After partaking of the elements, each family could then go immediately through the food serving line to begin the banquet aspect of the holy meal. This is an issue of freedom; adaptations can be made to suit the needs of each church.

Yeast

During Passover, the Jews ate unleavened bread to symbolize the speed with which God brought them out of Egypt. No doubt, Jesus used unleavened bread during the Last Supper. However, the New Testament is silent on the use of unleavened bread in Gentile churches. In the New Testament, yeast is sometimes associated with evil (1Co 5:6–8). It is also used to represent God's kingdom (Mt 13:33). The real symbolism is the bread itself, leavened or unleavened, as Jesus' body.

It is clear from 1 Corinthians 11 that wine was used in the Lord's Supper—some became drunk. However, no clear theological reason is given in the New Testament for its being alcoholic (consider Ge 27:28, Isa 25:6–9, and Ro 14:21). Jesus called it simply the fruit of the vine. The object lesson is that red wine looks like blood. As is the case with leavened or unleavened bread, the use of wine or grape juice would seem to be a matter of freedom. Thus, each local church can make decisions with spiritual sensitivity for one another.

Unbelievers

Most churches restrict access to the elements. For example, the *Baptist Faith and Message 2000* declared baptism by immersion as the prerequisite for enjoying the privileges of the Lord's Supper. However, the celebration of the Lord's Supper as a meal could change the perspective on the presence of unbelievers. That the bread and wine are only for believers should be announced. The Lord's Supper, as an actual meal, has spiritual significance to believers only. To nonbelievers, it is merely another meal. As is the case with believers, unbelieving adults and children who are too young to believe also experience hunger. They can be invited to enjoy the meal. We can love them to the Lord! The danger in taking the Lord's Supper in an "unworthy manner" applies only to believers (1Co 11:27–32).

Logistics

Sandra Atkerson contributed the following practical ideas on logistics: "Ask each family to prepare food at home and bring it to share with everyone else. Many churches have had great success with the potluck (or pot providence) method. The Lord's Supper is a feast of good and bountiful food with fellowship centered around Christ, a picture of the marriage banquet of the Lamb. It is a time to give and share liberally with our brothers and sisters in Christ. As for how much to bring, if you were having one more family over for dinner with your family, how much of one dish would you prepare? If church were canceled for some reason, could you satisfy your own family with what you prepared to take to the Lord's Supper? Encourage each family to bring a main dish and a side dish. Desserts should be considered optional and brought as a third dish but never as the only dish by a family. At least enough food should be brought by every family to feed themselves and have more left over to share with others. The singles, especially those not inclined to cook, might bring drinks, peanuts, dessert, chips and dip, or a prepared deli item such as potato salad or rotisserie chicken. The congregation should see this as a giving expense, a ministry, an offering to the Lord.

Confusion is minimized at the time of serving if your dish is ready when you arrive. Cook it before you come. Consider investing in a Pyrex Portables insulated hot/cold carrier that will keep your food at the temperature at which it was prepared. Hot plates can be plugged in to keep dishes warm. Others could bring crock pots. The oven can be put on warm and dishes stored there. Wool blankets or beach towels work well for hot/cold insulation during transport. Coolers in the summer months are great for icing down cold dishes.

The main point to remember for food safety is to keep hot foods hot at 150 degrees and cold foods cold at 40 degrees. Once the food is out for serving, it should sit out no longer than 2–3 hours before it is refrigerated. Dispose of any food left out longer than four hours.

Parents should consider helping their children prepare plates. Little ones often have eyes bigger than their stomachs and much food can go to waste. Many churches prefer to buy smaller 12-ounce cups. Most folks tend to fill their cups full, often not drinking it all. Smaller cups make less waste. It is better to go back for refills than to throw away unwanted drink.

A word about hygiene might be appropriate—there can never be enough hand washing among friends! Be sensitive to germs. All folks going through the serving line should wash before touching serving utensils. Put out a pump jar of hand sanitizer right by the plates at the beginning of the line. To help with cleanup, consider using paper plates and plastic cups and forks."[44]

NTRF.org has audio, video, articles, and a teacher's discussion guide on participatory church meetings.

---

[44]   Sandra Atkerson, "Hints for Hosting the Lord's Supper," NTRF.org. Accessed March 31, 2015.

Strategy #4

Servant Leaders Who Build Consensus

J esus said that church leaders have the same authority as children and slaves (those with the least authority in Roman society). He drove this truth home by washing the disciples' feet. Jesus even promised, "If you know these things, blessed are you if you do them." *What does this tell us about a church leader's management style, and about decision-making in church?*

Profit

A major component of Jesus' leadership strategy was for church leaders to serve the church by taking the time to build congregational consensus. This is very doable in a smaller congregation, but nearly impossible in larger churches. The mind of Christ is more likely to be found when the leaders guide the whole congregation to wrestle corporately with major decisions. Church members are encouraged when they realize that everyone's suggestions are respectfully weighed in accordance with Scripture. Unity is strengthened, and the church can more easily be guided by the Spirit. In this process, the role of the leadership includes helping to build consensus by teaching what Scripture says on an issue, having private conversations with church members about decisions, appealing to those who differ, and, after much persuasion, calling on any dissenting minority to yield to the leadership and the rest of the congregation. Adopting Jesus' example can make the church's decision-making process both unifying and edifying for the whole congregation.

Proof #1—The Authority of Church Leaders: As Children and

Slaves

Contrasting the authority of secular political leaders with that of church leaders, Jesus said: "The kings of the Gentiles exercise lordship over them, and those in authority over them are called benefactors. But not so with you. Rather, let the greatest among you become as the youngest, and the leader as one who serves" (Lk 22:25–26). Let us think about this for a minute. How much authority does the youngest person in a family have? How much authority does a household servant have over his employer? Although it is true that Jesus was a master of hyperbole, there is an underlying truth that must not be glossed over. Church leaders are to be servant leaders. Their attitude should be one of humility in leadership: not kingly authority that lords it over others. Church leaders must lead with a servant's heart. In harmony with Jesus' words, Peter instructed elders to "shepherd the flock of God ... not domineering over those in your charge, but being examples to the flock" (1Pt 5:1–3).[1]

---

[1] The New Testament uses the words pastor, elder, and overseer (or bishop) interchangeably without any hierarchical ranking (Acts 20:17, 28, Titus 1:5–7, 1 Pt 5:1–3). They are synonymous terms.

"I Have Given You an Example"

Jesus offered Himself as an example for church leaders to follow: "Who is the greater, one who reclines at table or one who serves? Is it not the one who reclines at table? But I am among you as the one who serves" (Lk 22:27). On another occasion, Jesus washed the disciples' feet to make the point that anyone who wants to be a church leader must first learn to be the servant of all. He said: "Do you understand what I have done to you? You call me Teacher and Lord, and you are right, for so I am. If I then, your Lord and Teacher, have washed your feet, you also ought to wash one another's feet. For I have given you an example, that you also should do just as I have done to you. Truly, truly, I say to you, a servant is not greater than his master, nor is a messenger greater than the one who sent him. If you know these things, blessed are you if you do them" (Jn 13:12–17). Do we want to receive God's blessing as church leaders? Then we must live out what Jesus modeled and wield our authority with a servant's heart.

Proof #2—Elder Rule Properly Understood

Because Scripture mentions elders who "rule well" (1Ti 5:17), it is obvious that God intended for church leaders to serve in a management capacity. The word underlying "rule" literally means "to stand before," i.e., directing or managing others. A secondary meaning is to stand before in the sense of caring for or giving aid to others as would a nurse or attending physician.[2] Combining these two definitions helps to frame the management style that is to be employed by church leaders.

Obey Your Leaders

How can someone who has only the authority of children or slaves be expected to rule? Hebrews 13:17 instructs believers to *obey* church leaders.[3] The common Greek word for "obey" (*hupakouo*) was used to

---

[2] *Proistémi*, Bauer, *Lexicon*, 707.

[3] The New Testament usually refers to church leaders in the plural. Only one leader in a congregation was foreign to the early church.

refer to situations such as children obeying their parents and slaves their masters (Eph 6:1, 5). However, the common word for "obey" is not found in 13:17. Instead, *peitho*, which fundamentally means persuade or convince, is used.[4] In Greek mythology, "Peitho" was the name of a goddess, a consort of Aphrodite, who personified persuasion.[5] Consistent with this root meaning, McReynolds' interlinear translation of *peitho* in 13:17 is "persuade."[6] One expositor went a step further and stated that with *peitho*, "the obedience suggested is not by submission to authority, but resulting from persuasion."[7] Lenski's comment on this text was that those who allow themselves to be convinced by someone would obey that person.[8] In our passage, it is found in the present imperative middle/passive form, which means "obey."[9] However, the author's use of *peitho* suggests that this obedience is born of dialog, teaching, persuasion, and argument. Mindless obedience is not what is envisioned. Someone who is persuaded of something will act on it, obeying it with joyful conviction.

Persuasion

One of the qualifications of an elder is the ability to teach (1Ti 3:2). This is because church leaders have to persuade by teaching the truth. Dwight Eisenhower captured the idea behind Hebrews 13:17 when he said: "I would rather try to persuade a man to go along, because once I have persuaded him, he will stick. If I scare him, he will stay just as long as he is scared, and then he is gone."[10] Elders are not to simply pronounce decisions from on high like popes. The servant leader

---

[4] Bauer, *Lexicon*, 639. Other examples of *peitho* are found in Luke 16:31 and Acts 17:4 and 21:14.

[5] "Peitho," en.Wikipedia.org. Accessed October 5, 2017.

[6] Paul McReynolds, *Word Study Greek–English New Testament* (Wheaton: Tyndale, 1999), 819.

[7] W.E. Vine, *Expository Dictionary of New Testament Words* (Iowa Falls: Riverside Book & Bible House, 1952), 124.

[8] R. C. H. Lenski, *Interpretation of the Epistle to the Hebrews and the Epistle of James* (Minneapolis: Augsburg Publishing, 1966), 490.

[9] Horst Balz & Gerhard Schneider, eds., *Exegetical Dictionary of the New Testament*, Vol. 3 (Grand Rapids: Eerdmans, 1993), 63.

[10] QuotationsPage.com, #2662, accessed September 30, 2016.

sells instead of tells. Ideally, the obedience described in Hebrews 13:17 will happen after a process of persuasion.

Submit to Your Leaders

Hebrews 13:17 further instructs believers to *submit* to their church leaders. However, the common Greek word for "submit" (*hupotasso*) is not found here.[11] Instead, the classical Greek word *hupeiko*, a synonym for *hupotasso*, which means to yield or to give way, was chosen by the author.[12] Rienecker defined it more precisely as "to give in, to yield, to submit."[13] *Hupeiko* was used elsewhere with reference to contestants (such as wrestlers) and meant to yield after a struggle.[14] The nuanced understanding *hupeiko* is not that of a structure, such as civil government, to which someone automatically submits; rather, it is submission at the end of a process, struggle, or contest. It is a portrait of serious discussion and dialogue prior to one party's giving way.

Section Summary

In summary, the relationship presented in the New Testament is not mindless slave-like obedience between leaders and those who are led. God's flock must be open to being persuaded (*peitho*) by their shepherds. Leaders, in turn, must be committed to ongoing teaching and discussion. However, there will be times when someone or a few in the fellowship cannot be persuaded. Congregations are made up of both mature and immature Christians, of those who walk in the Spirit and those who do not, of those with the gift of discernment and those without it. Impasses will arise. Hebrews 13:17 calls on dissenters, after much persuasion, to yield (*hupeiko*) to the wisdom of their church leaders. This submission, however, is to come only after dialogue, discussion, and reasoning. Thus, even though final decision-making authority

---

[11]   Used, for example, in Romans 13:1, Colossians 3:18, Ephesians 5:21, and 1 Peter 2:13.

[12]   Bauer, *Lexicon*, 838.

[13]   Rienecker, *Linguistic Key*, 720.

[14]   "hupeiko", BibleStudyTools.org. Accessed February 25, 2021.

resides with the leadership, a critical aspect of elder rule must include a commitment to serve the Body by building Spirit-led congregational consensus. Just as a person can have an opinion without being opinionated or make judgments without being judgmental, so too a leader has authority to rule without being authoritarian.

Proof #3—Church Leaders: Star Players or Sideline Coaches?

Amazingly, church leaders were given little prominence in the epistles. Paul's highly theological epistle to the Romans was addressed simply to the "saints" (Ro 1:7), with no special mention of the shepherds. The two letters to the Corinthian congregation were addressed to the whole "church" (1Co 1:2; 2Co 1:1). There was no mention of the leaders in either the greetings or anywhere else in the body of the letters. That these two epistles deal with critical leadership topics such as the Lord's Supper, worship services, and church discipline makes this all the more remarkable.

Galatians, Ephesians, Philippians, Colossians

The greeting in Galatians was to all the "churches" in the region. No mention was made of the leadership (1:2). Throughout Galatians, the readers were addressed simply as "brothers." The "saints in Ephesus" were the designated recipients of their letter (Eph 1:1). The importance of pastor-teachers was mentioned in Ephesians 4:11, but even there the leaders were not written to directly. Philippians 1:1 breaks the pattern of leadership neglect. The overseers were greeted along with the saints. However, no other mention was made of these leaders, nor was anything else written directly to them. The salutation in Colossians 1:2 was simply to "the saints and faithful brothers." Nothing was written directly to or about the leaders. In the last chapter of Hebrews, the readers were asked to "greet all your leaders" (13:24). Not only did the author not greet the leaders directly, but he assumed they would not even read the letter.

Thessalonians, James, Peter, John, Jude

This failure to focus on the leaders continues in the salutations of 1& 2 Thessalonians, James, 1& 2 Peter, 1 & 2 John,[15] and Jude. Of all the letters to the churches, it is only in 1 Peter 5 that elders are written to directly.[16] None of this should be taken to mean that church leaders are unimportant. It is simply that shepherds are themselves sheep too. The leaders were a subset of the church as a whole. There was no strong clergy–laity distinction. Ephesians 4:11–12 reveals that the duty of pastor-teachers is to equip the saints for the work of the ministry. This, combined with the apostolic spotlight on entire congregations rather than just the leadership, suggests that leaders are to serve as sideline coaches rather than star players.

Direct Appeals to Entire Congregations

Much may be gleaned from the New Testament writers' direct appeals to entire congregations. They went to great lengths to influence all believers—not just those in leadership. The apostles did not simply bark out orders or issue injunctions as military commanders might do. Instead, they treated other believers as equals and appealed directly to them. The priesthood of the believer was actively practiced. Local church leaders no doubt led in much the same way. Their primary authority was in their ability to influence through the truth. The respect they were given was earned honestly. It was the opposite of military authority wherein soldiers respect the uniform but not necessarily the man. Aristotle astutely stated: "We believe good men more fully and more readily than others. This is true generally whatever the question is, and absolutely true where exact certainty is impossible and opinions are divided ... his character may almost be called the most effective

---

[15] 3 John was written to Gaius, a church leader, rather than an entire congregation.

[16] The letters to Timothy and Titus are referred to as "pastoral epistles" because of their emphasis on pastors. However, Timothy and Titus were not local church leaders. They were apostolic workers sent by Paul to various places to organize churches.

means of persuasion he possesses."[17]

Lead By Example

Hebrews 13:7 reflects the fact that the leadership style employed by church leaders is primarily one of direction by example: "Remember your leaders.... Consider the outcome of their way of life and imitate their faith." Similarly, 1 Thessalonians 5:13 reveals that leaders are to be respected not because of the automatic authority of appointed rank but because of the value of their service: "esteem them very highly in love because of their work." As Jesus said: "You know that the rulers of the Gentiles lord it over them, and their high officials exercise authority over them. Not so with you. Instead, whoever wants to become great among you must be your servant, and whoever wants to be first must be your slave" (Mt 20:25–27).

Section Summary

In summary, the Apostles wrote to entire churches and not just the leadership. The Apostles taught, gave reasons, persuaded, and guided as opposed to merely issuing orders. Servant leaders should serve by leading in this manner. Leaders are to be great in service.

Proof #4—Church As Congress

We will have a poorer understanding of Christ's church if we fail to factor in the dynamics of the original Greek word for church: *ek-klésia*. With so much emphasis today on the separation of church and state, government is seldom associated with the church. However, in Jesus' day, *ekklésia* was used outside the New Testament to refer to a political assembly that was regularly convened for the purpose of making decisions.[18] According to Thayer, it was "an assembly of the

---

[17]   *Aristotle's Rhetoric*, Book 1, Chapter 2.

[18]   In the Scriptures, *ekklésia* was also used to refer to a gathering of Israel, to the church as the totality of Christians living in one location, and to the universal church to which all believers belong.

people convened at the public place of council for the purpose of deliberation."[19] Bauer defines *ekklésia* as an "assembly of a regularly summoned political body."[20] Writing for *The New International Dictionary of New Testament Theology*, Lothan Coenen noted that *ekklésia* was "clearly characterized as a political phenomenon, repeated according to certain rules and within a certain framework. It was the assembly of full citizens, functionally rooted in the constitution of the democracy, an assembly in which fundamental political and judicial decisions were taken ... the word *ekklésia*, throughout the Greek and Hellenistic areas, always retained its reference to the assembly of the polis."[21]

Legal Assembly

The secular meaning of *ekklésia* can be seen several times in Acts 19, where it is translated as "legal assembly" rather than "church."[22] Two of the occurrences in Acts 19 refer to a meeting of silversmiths convened by Demetrius. These trade union members rushed into the theater where civic decisions were normally made in order to decide what to do about a damaged reputation and lost business.[23] However, they overstepped their jurisdiction, so the town clerk counseled that the matter be settled by the "legal" *ekklésia* rather than the trade union *ekklésia* (Acts 19:37–39).

A Decision-Making Mandate

Why did Jesus choose such a politically loaded word (*ekklésia*) to describe His people and their meetings?[24] Had He merely wanted to describe a gathering with no political connotations, Jesus could have used

---

[19] Thayer, *Lexicon*, 196.

[20] Bauer, *Lexicon*, 240.

[21] Lothan Coenen, "Church," *New International Dictionary of New Testament Theology*, Vol. 1, Colin Brown, General Editor (Grand Rapids: Zondervan, 1971), 291.

[22] Acts 19:32, 39, 41 (NIV).

[23] "Theater," Ephesus.us, accessed September 1, 2016. There was so much confusion that a majority did not know why they had been summoned.

[24] Matthew 16:13–20 & 18:15–20. In the *Septuagint*, wilderness gatherings of the ancient Israelites were called *ekklésia*.

sunagogé. Perhaps it was because Jesus intended His followers to function together with a purpose that parallels that of the political government. If so, believers have the responsibility to make decisions together through consensus. God's people have a decision-making mandate. A church is a body of Kingdom citizens authorized to weigh major issues, to make decisions, and to pass judgment on various issues. The *Baptist Faith and Message* of 2000 stated: "Each congregation operates under the Lordship of Christ through democratic processes."[25]

The Keys of the Kingdom

The New Testament contains many examples of God's people making decisions as a body. After promising to build His *ekklésia* on the rock of Peter's revealed confession, Jesus immediately spoke of the keys to the kingdom of heaven and of binding and loosing (Mt 16:13–20). Keys symbolize the authority to open and to close something. "Kingdom" is a political term, and binding and loosing involve the authority to make decisions. Was this authority given to Peter only? In Matthew 18:15–20, the authority to bind and loose was conferred on the whole *ekklésia* by Jesus. In Acts 1:15–26, Peter charged the Jerusalem church as a whole with finding a replacement for Judas. Later, the apostles looked to the church corporately to choose men to administer the church's food program (Acts 6:1–6). Acts 14:23 indicates that the apostles appointed elders with the wide agreement of the local congregation.[26]

Jerusalem Council

The Apostles were the standard for doctrine and practice. If ever there were an appropriate time and place for the Apostles to make a decision on their own apart from the church, it would have been the Jerusalem Council (Acts 15). The very nature of the Gospel had been

---

[25] Article VI, "The Church."
[26] "Paul and Barnabas had elders elected" (footnoted alternative translation, NIV).

called into question. Yet, even here, the amazing fact is that the Apostles included not only the local Jerusalem elders but also the whole church.[27] Colin Brown observed: "In the council's decision-making they are accorded no special preeminence.... It is consistent with the non-authoritarian, collegiate character of church leadership which Acts consistently depicts (1:13–26; 6:2ff; 8:14ff; 11:1ff; 13:1–4)."[28] Servant leadership is decentralized. Furthermore, 1 Corinthians 5 reveals that the church corporately has the authority to lovingly discipline unrepentant members.

Professors

Commenting on the general nature of congregational involvement, Donald Guthrie observed: "These early communities displayed a remarkable virility, which was a particular characteristic of that age. The churches were living organisms rather than organizations. The promptings of the Spirit were more important than ecclesiastical edicts or Episcopal pronouncements. When decisions were made, they were made by the whole company of believers, not simply by the officials.... It would be a mistake, nevertheless, to suppose because of this that the church was run on democratic lines. The Acts record makes unmistakably clear that the dominating factor was the guidance of the Holy Spirit."[29]

Guthrie further said: "Any examination of Paul's view of the leadership within the Christian community must begin from his basic idea that the church is a body of which Christ is the head. No authority structure is possible without the supreme authority being vested in Christ Himself. Moreover, even here the authority must be understood as organic and not organizational ... it is the most intimate kind of authority.... Any officials who are mentioned must be regarded as exercising

---

[27] Acts 15:4, 12, 22.

[28] Brown, Vol. 1, *Dictionary*, 135.

[29] Guthrie, *Theology*, 741.

their various functions under the direction of the head.... Although the Christian church is not a democracy, neither is it an autocracy. Indeed, the one instance mentioned in the NT where one man sought to lord it over the community is regarded with strong disfavor (3 John 9–10). The NT idea of the church is a community in which Christ, not man, is the head (Col. 1:18; Eph. 1:22). It is theocratic, not democratic. Its sense of law and order is dominated by God's will (cf. 1 Cor. 5:3–5)."[30]

Section Summary

The New Testament approach is for leaders to involve the whole church in major decisions, relying on the Holy Spirit's guidance and seeking to build congregational consensus on important matters. Early church government was a combination of elder rule and congregational consensus under Christ as the Head. If the church leaned too much in one direction, it would become a dictatorship, and too much in the other, there would be mob rule. The leaders and the church are in a nuanced dance of mutual respect as they look to Jesus as the Head, the caller of the dance steps.

Provision

The process a church goes through to achieve consensus can be just as important as the consensus that is finally achieved. Consensus governing takes time, commitment, mutual edification, and a great deal of brotherly love. It truly *can* work in smaller churches, such as those in the New Testament era.[31] We must love enough to accept one another and to work through our disagreements. The concept of consensus could be called government by unity, oneness, harmony, or mutual agreement. Do we really trust in the Holy Spirit to work in our lives and churches?

---

[30]   Ibid., 760 & 946.

[31]   Because the early church met in the private homes of its wealthier members, each congregation was necessarily small (scores of people rather than hundreds or thousands).

The Lord's Prayer

It is important to consider what the Lord has done to help His people. First, our Lord Himself prayed "that they may be one as we are one ... that all of them may be one, Father, just as you are in me and I am in you.... May they be brought into complete unity" (Jn 17:11, 21–23). Because Jesus asked this on our behalf, unity is certainly achievable.

The Lord's Supper

Another provision God made for our unity lies in the Lord's Supper: "Because there is one loaf, we, who are many, are one body, for we all partake of the one loaf" (1Co 10:17). The prepositions "because" and "for" are important. Partaking of the Lord's Supper not only symbolizes unity, but it even creates it.[32]

The Lord's Leaders

Finally, Christ gave the church various leadership gifts (such as pastor-teacher) for a purpose: "until we all reach unity in the faith" (Eph 4:11–13). Leaders play a critical role in building consensus.

Proposition

Jesus said that church leaders are to become like children and slaves: those with the least authority in worldly Roman society. Jesus Himself came not as a king but as a servant. A servant leader is concerned about the needs and desires of others, truly respects the values and dignity of the brethren, believes in and practices the priesthood of the believer, adopts a participative management style, and takes the time and effort to build congregational consensus in problem-solving and decision-making. Serving in this way involves shepherding, community-building, making disciples, teaching, persuasion, listening,

---

[32] See Chapter 1 for more details.

explanation, empathy, humility, and coaching.

The church as a whole may be compared to a congress with authority to make decisions and to render judgments that are binding on its members. Church leaders are congressmen as well. However, they are appointed to a special committee whose purpose is to study the issues and to make recommendations, teach, inform, or prompt the congress. Church leaders should not normally make decisions on behalf of the church as an alternative to seeking consensus. Leaders should guide, teach, suggest, and build consensus. However, when the church finds itself in gridlock, unable to resolve an issue, the leaders serve as predetermined arbitrators or tiebreakers. In these instances, those in opposition are called on to submit in the Lord to the elders' leadership and wisdom (Heb 13:17). Spirit-filled elder rule, combined with congregational consensus on major decisions, gives free rein to the Holy Spirit and puts the church in a better position to discern the mind of Christ and to walk in the Light of God's Word.

Practicum

Should decisions be made by consensus or simple majority? It is important to consider what is implied in these two options. Consensus means general agreement, a representative trend, or an opinion. Related words are "consent" and "consensual." In contrast, majority rule can be a 51% dictatorship for the 49% who do not agree. This works against unity. Consensus, however, seeks to build unity.

No Divisions: Consider the following biblical texts: "How good and pleasant it is when brothers live together in unity" (Ps 133:1). "I appeal to you, brothers, in the name of our Lord Jesus Christ, that all of you agree with one another so that there may be no divisions among you and that you may be perfectly united in mind and thought" (1Co 1:10). "Make every effort to keep the unity of the Spirit through the bond of peace" (Eph 4:3). "Make my joy complete by being like-minded, having the same love, being one in spirit and purpose" (Php 2:2). "Clothe yourselves with compassion, kindness, humility, gentleness, and patience. Bear with each other and forgive whatever grievances you may have against one another. Forgive as the Lord forgave you. And over all these virtues put on love, which binds them all together in perfect unity" (Col 3:12–15).

Building Consensus: Systematic, well-presented, biblically-based teaching that is soaked in fervent prayer will facilitate mature discussion. Even though leaders will bring teachings that are relevant to the issues under consideration in church meetings, much of the consensus-building process will occur outside a church service. It will happen one-on-one, brother to brother in many ways, including the fellowship of the Lord's Supper, midweek social visits, telephone conversations, text messages, and email. Bringing church members into agreement requires time, patience, humility, gentleness, and the ministry of elders. There is a major difference between consensus and simple majority rule, which involves voting and a 51% "win."

Congregational Voting: In the consensus process, there may never be a time that a vote is taken. The leadership should know each brother's position on the basis of individual conversations. Due consideration should be given to the opinions of godly, mature, longstanding members rather than those who have just begun to attend. After consensus has been reached and any few remaining dissenters have been asked to yield to the elders, an announcement can be made and the proposal implemented.

Should a general meeting of the church be held to ascertain whether there is consensus on an issue? Ideally, the church should be small enough that the leadership knows where each person stands without necessarily having to call a general meeting. However, it would be appropriate to have special meetings, apart from worship services, for teaching about and discussing important issues.

Who makes decisions in the consensus process? Should it be men and women or only men? Everyone's thoughts are important. In the Trinity, God the Father and God the Son are equal; however, the Son voluntarily submits to the Father's will. Even though men and women are equal in God's sight, wives are called on to submit to their husbands. God is the head of Christ, Christ is the head of the church, and the husband is the head of his family. One way this divine order is expressed in the church is that only men are to serve as elders and teachers. It is further expressed when men, as heads of their homes, represent their wives' opinions in the consensus process. Certainly, wives have valid opinions and insights. These concerns may be expressed directly by the women or through their husbands. A loving husband will carefully consider his wife's views, but it is the brothers who have the last say. It is the brothers who must make the decisions that are binding on the church (See 1Co 11:1ff, 14:33–35; 1Ti 2:11–15).

In matters of mere preference, being considerate of the women and yielding to their desires is the appropriate course to take. However, in matters of theology or the application of Scripture, the men must make the final decisions. In his commentary on 1 Corinthians 14:33–35, R.C.H. Lenski quoted from an *Opinion of the Theological Faculty of Capital University*: "How the granting of voice and vote to women in all congregational meetings can do anything but place women completely on a level with men in all such meetings and gravely interfere with their divinely ordered subjection and obedience, we are unable to see."[33]

When do issues rise to a level that requires consensus? It is impractical to involve the entire church in every decision. The key is to

---

[33] R.C.H. Lenski, *Interpretation of I & II Corinthians* (Minneapolis: Augsburg Publishing House, 1943), 617.

focus on achieving consensus on major issues, such as large purchases, selecting elders and deacons, church discipline, determining the location for the church to meet, making significant changes to the way meetings are conducted, planting new churches, supporting missionaries, or starting outreach ministries.

When does the size of the congregation present a problem? No magic number is provided in the Scriptures for the optimal congregational size. If a church is too big for the elders to know and have a relationship with every man, it is too big. Consensus governing works best in a congregation that is small enough for everyone to know and love one another. Relationships must be strong enough to allow people to work through their disagreements without becoming upset and leaving the church. It is noteworthy that the early church met in Roman villas. The typical villa could accommodate approximately 100 people.[34]

What about inactive or newly converted members? Do their voices count in the consensus process? There will almost always be spiritually immature people in a church. The opinions of the inactive should carry the same weight as their involvement with the church. This is precisely where Hebrews 13:17 is relevant. After reasonable discussions and appeals, such persons are to listen and yield to the wisdom of the elders.

How should consensus apply to interpretations of the Bible? Certainly, we should study the Bible as individuals but not individualistically. We need to weigh our interpretations against the consensus of the Church: not just our local church but the Church universal. Historical humility is needed. To reject the time-honored conclusions of millions of our fellow believers over thousands of years is to effectively become little popes who fancy themselves as having the divine right to

---

[34] To read more on size considerations, see Chapter 5.

interpret Scripture autonomously.[35]

Regula Fidei: The Scriptures teach that the Holy Spirit dwells in every believer. As we survey the beliefs of the Church around the world today and throughout the past two millennia, we can readily see several fundamental agreements about the correct interpretation of Scripture. This has to be more than coincidence. It is the work of the Spirit. Some of these general agreements are about matters such as the virgin birth, the Trinity, the deity of Christ, the propitiatory nature of Christ's death on the cross, the bodily resurrection of Christ, the future bodily return of Christ, the future bodily resurrection of the dead, and the inspiration of Scripture. When the church universal has arrived at a consensus about a doctrine, it becomes authoritative. Does one congregation have the right to defy the historical consensus of the church? These basic agreed-upon doctrines constitute the *regula fidei*, the rule of faith. We need a good dose of historical humility.

Democracy of the Dead: Thus, we can see that there are limits to what a local church as a decision-making body should determine. No local church has a license to redefine the historical Christian faith. Some doctrines are simply not open for debate. Each *ekklésia* should operate within the bounds of orthodoxy. The elders are to consider the harmful and heretical ideas to be off limits (1Ti 1:3). The reason is that the church at large today and throughout time has already reached a consensus on certain fundamental interpretations of Scripture. The Holy Spirit has not failed in His mission of guiding the church into all truth (Jn 16:13). G. K. Chesterton said: "Tradition means giving votes to the most obscure of all classes, our ancestors. It is the democracy of the dead. Tradition refuses to submit to the small and arrogant oligarchy of those who merely happen to be walking about."[36]

---

[35] Keith Mathison, *The Shape of Sola Scriptura* (Moscow: Canon Press, 2001).

[36] "Tradition Is the Democracy of the Dead," Chesterton.org, accessed September 1, 2016.

Plural Leadership: New Testament references to local church leaders are generally in the plural. For example: "they had appointed elders for them in every church" (Acts 14:23), and "call for the elders of the church" (Jam 5:14). From such texts, many have inferred that each local church should have a plurality of elders. Generally, each church should have as many men as are qualified to serve as elders. Ideally, it should be a plurality.[37] The following are some of the benefits of plural leadership:

1. The chances of a dictatorship developing are reduced. We should remember Lord Acton's wise words: "Power tends to corrupt, and absolute power corrupts absolutely. Great men are almost always bad men." Even if only one brother is qualified to serve as an elder, an understanding that elder rule is to include consensus building among all the brothers will help to avoid the development of a modern Diotrephes: "I have written something to the church, but Diotrephes, who likes to put himself first, does not acknowledge our authority. So if I come, I will bring up what he is doing, talking wicked nonsense against us. And not content with that, he refuses to welcome the brothers, and also stops those who want to and puts them out of the church" (3Jn 1:9–10).

2. Dealing with an attack of wolves is easier: "I know that after my departure fierce wolves will come in among you, not sparing the flock; and from among your own selves will arise men speaking twisted things, to draw away the disciples after them" (Acts 20:29–30). Ecclesiastes 4:12 says: "Though one may be overpowered, two can defend themselves. A cord of three strands is not quickly broken."

3. There is greater wisdom: "By wise guidance you can wage

---

[37] As to the difference between an elder, overseer (KJV: "bishop"), and pastor (shepherd), an examination of Acts 20:17, 28–30, Titus 1:5–7, and 1 Peter 5:1–3 will show synonymous usage.

your war, and in abundance of counselors there is victory"
(Pr 24:6).

4. As reflected in Jethro's advice to Moses (Ex 18:13–27),
having several elders would allow for the sharing of the work-
load, e.g., hospital visitation, teaching, counseling, and dealing with problems.

5. It taps into a broader range of spiritual gifts. Elders do not
have the same gifts or motivations: "Let the elders who rule
well be considered worthy of double honor, especially those
who labor in preaching and teaching" (1Ti 5:17).

6. It has been said that it is lonely at the top. Being a sole
elder can be lonely and discouraging. Having several elders
makes for mutual encouragement.

Discussion Questions

1. What can Luke 22:24–27 teach about a church leader's authority?

2. To what did the Greek word *ekklésia* originally refer?

3. Why did Jesus choose a political word such as *ekklésia* to describe
His followers?

4. What are some New Testament examples of God's people making
decisions as a body?

5. What is the difference between majority rule and congregational
consensus?

6. What is the difference between consensus and unanimity?

7. What provisions has God made to help a church achieve consensus?

8. How do leaders build congregational consensus?

9. In Hebrews 13:17, believers are encouraged to obey and submit to
their leaders. How does this square with congregational rule?

*NTRF.org has audio, video, articles, and a teacher's discussion
guide on participatory church meetings.*

Strategy #5

Small Congregations for Effective Shepherding

Wen it comes to congregational size, it's easy to assume that bigger is better. *But is it really? Instead of one thousand people in a single church, might it be better to have them spread out in ten churches?* For its first two-hundred years, the church met illegally and secretly in the private homes of its members. The typical pastor was bi-vocational. Since every New Testament church letter was written to a congregation that met in a home, the ecclesiology presented in the epistles was designed for effective shepherding in smaller settings. Using these church practices, God's kingdom spread like yeast throughout the Roman Empire. Bigger isn't necessarily better—*better* is better! Smaller churches have strategic, divinely-designed size advantages for pastoral effective ministry.

Profit

Sixty percent of all Protestant churches in the United States have fewer than 100 adults attending.[1] Over 40,000 Southern Baptist Churches fall into this category.[2] Our premise is that good things really do come in small packages. Smaller settings can foster the simplicity, intimacy, unity, love, support, and accountability that characterized the early church. The relationships described in the New Testament work best in situations in which everyone knows everyone else. A loving, family-like atmosphere is more easily developed. The many "one another" exhortations of Scripture can be more realistically lived out. Church discipline takes on genuine significance. Disciple-making is natural and personal. Participatory meetings are better suited for smaller settings. Celebrating the Lord's Supper with the *Agapé* love feast is more natural in a smaller, family-like setting. Achieving congregational consensus is easier when everyone knows everyone else and open lines of communication genuinely exist. Involvement with a smaller church can be a wonderful blessing with strategic, divinely-designed advantages.

Little Congregations

Charles Spurgeon opined: "It strikes me that there would be a great deal of good done if persons who have large rooms in their houses would endeavor to get together little congregations .... Where there is a Church in the house, every member strives to increase the other's comfort, all seek to promote each other's holiness, each one endeavors to discharge his duty according to the position in which he is placed in that Church."[3]

Assemble in Some Home

No less a Reformation luminary than Martin Luther wrote:

---

[1] "Small Churches Struggle to Grow Because of the People They Attract," Barna.org, accessed August 26, 2016.

[2] Personal conversation with Johnny Hunt of the North American Mission Board.

[3] Charles Spurgeon, "A Pastoral Visit," ccel.org. Accessed Sept 4, 2020.

"Those ... desirous of being Christians in earnest ... should ... assemble by themselves in some house ... those whose conduct was not such as befits Christians could be recognized, reproved ... or excommunicated.... Here we could have baptism and the sacrament ... and direct everything towards the Word and prayer and love...." Smaller churches have strategic, divinely-designed size advantages for effective ministry.

Proof

According to Yale University archaeologists: "The first Christian congregations worshipped in private houses, meeting at the homes of wealthier members on a rotating basis.... Worship was generally conducted in the atrium, or central courtyard of the house." [4] For example Philemon, who was wealthy enough to own a slave, hosted a church in his home (Phlm 2b). Church hostess Lydia was a prosperous business-woman who sold expensive purple fabric and could afford household servants (Acts 16:14). Churches met in the various homes of Aquila and Priscilla, a couple involved in the evidently lucrative first-century tent-making trade (Acts 18:1–3).[5] Gaius had a home big enough to host the sizable Corinthian congregation (1Co 1:14; Ro 16:23).

No Buildings Before Constantine

Less well known is the fact that the early church continued the practice of home meetings for hundreds of years after the apostolic era. Graydon Snyder of Chicago Theological Seminary observed: "The New Testament Church began as a small group house church (Col. 4:15), and it remained so until the middle or end of the third century. There are no evidences of larger places of meeting before 300."[6] Snyder also stated: "There is no literary evidence nor archaeological indication that

---

[4] "Unearthing the Christian Building," *Dura-Europos: Excavating Antiquity* (Yale University Art Gallery), 2.

[5] Through his tent making, Paul was able to support not only himself but also his traveling companions (at least seven men Acts 20:4, 34).

[6] Snyder, *Church Life*, 166.

any such home was converted into an extant church building. Nor is there any extant church that certainly was built prior to Constantine."[7]

The Ideal Size

The real issue is not where a church meets but how it can best do what God requires of it. Size plays an important role. Having too many people in attendance can defeat the purpose of holding a local church meeting. Large crowds are great for occasional praise concerts, teaching (Mt 4:25-5:1), or evangelism (Acts 5:12-14, 19). Such meetings are necessarily relatively impersonal. However, the weekly local church gathering is supposed to offer such personalized benefits as mutual edification, accountability, community, and fellowship. In keeping with the New Testament example, the ideal size for a congregation might be the number of people who would fit in a first-century Roman villa.[8] Smaller churches have strategic, divinely-designed size advantages for effective ministry.

Professors

Regarding the meeting places of early church meetings, Reformed scholar William Hendriksen said: "Since in the first and second centuries church buildings in the sense in which we think of them today were not yet in existence, families would hold services in their own homes."[9] Anglican priest and evangelist David Watson stated: "For the first two centuries, the church met in small groups in the homes of its members, apart from special gatherings in public lecture halls or market places, where people could come together in much larger numbers. Significantly, these two centuries mark the most powerful and vigorous

---

[7]   Ibid., 67.

[8]   Acts 16:40, 20:20; Ro 16:3–5a, 16:23; 1Co 16:19; Col 4:15; Phlm 1–2b; Jam 2:3. Though Scripture never states this, it is possible that churches also met in tenement housing, *insula*, which were not as large as the Roman villas.

[9]   William Hendriksen, "Exposition of Paul's Epistle to the Romans," *New Testament Commentary* (Grand Rapids: Baker, 1980), 22.

advance of the church, which perhaps has never been equaled."[10]

Martin Selman of Spurgeon's College in London wrote: "The theme of the 'household of God' undoubtedly owed much to the function of the house in early Christianity as a place of meeting and fellowship (e.g., 2 Tim. 4:19; Phm. 2; 2 Jn. 10)."[11] W. H. Griffith Thomas, co-founder of the Dallas Theological Seminary, opined: "For two or three centuries, Christians met in private houses…. There seems little doubt that these informal gatherings of small groups of believers had great influence in preserving the simplicity and purity of early Christianity."[12]

Seminary professor Ronald Sider concluded: "The early church was able to defy the decadent values of Roman civilization precisely because it experienced the reality of Christian fellowship in a mighty way…. Christian fellowship meant unconditional availability to and unlimited liability for the other sisters and brothers—emotionally, financially and spiritually. When one member suffered, they all suffered. When one rejoiced, they all rejoiced (1 Cor. 12:26). When a person or church experienced economic trouble, the others shared without reservation. And when a brother or sister fell into sin, the others gently restored the straying person (Mt. 18:15–17; 1 Cor. 5; 2 Cor. 2:5–11; Gal. 6:1–3). The sisters and brothers were available to each other, liable for each other and accountable to each other. The early church, of course, did not always fully live out the New Testament vision of the body of Christ. There were tragic lapses. But the network of tiny house churches scattered throughout the Roman Empire did experience their oneness in Christ so vividly that they were able to defy and eventually conquer a powerful, pagan civilization. The overwhelming majority of churches today, however, do not provide the context in which brothers

---

[10]   David Watson, *I Believe in the Church* (Great Britain: Hodder & Stoughton, 1978), 121.

[11]   Martin Selman, "House," *New Bible Dictionary*, ed. J. D. Douglas (Wheaton: Tyndale, 1982), 498.

[12]   W. H. Griffith Thomas, *St. Paul's Epistle to the Romans* (Grand Rapids: Eerdmans, 1984), 422–423.

and sisters can encourage, admonish and disciple each other. We desperately need new settings and structures for watching over one another in love."[13] Smaller churches have strategic, divinely-designed size advantages for effective ministry.

Pattern

What are we to do with the fact that the early church met mostly in homes? The most common explanation for the existence of early house churches was the pressure of persecution. Their situation was similar to that in China or Iran today. However, even without persecution, might the apostles have intended to lay out a purposeful pattern for smaller congregations? It is a design axiom that form follows function. Meeting in a smaller setting would have a practical effect on an individual's church life. The apostles' belief about the *function* of the church was naturally expressed in the first-century *form* of the church. Some distinct practices of those early small churches are worth considering:[14]

The Church as Family

The overarching significance of the New Testament church lies in its theology of community. Apostolic writers used words pertaining to family to describe the church. Believers are God's children (1Jn 3:1) who have been born into His spiritual family (Jn 1:12–13). God's people are thus seen as part of His household (Eph 2:19; Gal 6:10). They are called brothers and sisters (Phlm 2; Ro 16:2). Consequently, Christians are to relate to one another as members of a family (1Ti 5:1–2; Ro 16:13). Out of the theological truth that God's children are a spiritual family arise many issues surrounding church practices. This includes the congregation size that best facilitates functioning as God's family. According to Fuller seminary professor Robert Banks: "Even the meetings of the 'whole church' were small enough for a relatively inti-

---

[13] Ronald Sider, *Rich Christians in an Age of Hunger* (Downers Grove: Intervarsity, 1977), 190–191.
[14] Special thanks to Stephen David of Hyderabad, India for significant contributions to this section.

mate relationship to develop between the members."[15]

One-Another Ministry

The Scriptures are full of "one another" commands.[16] A church should be characterized by mutual encouragement, accountability, interpersonal relationships, community, and church discipline. These ideals are best accomplished in smaller congregations where people know and love one another. They will not be easily achieved in a large auditorium filled with people who are relative strangers. Nominal Christianity is harbored in settings where it is easy to get lost in the crowd. Smaller churches can best foster the simplicity, vitality, intimacy, and purity that God desires for His Church.

"Each One Has" Church Meetings

Early church meetings were clearly participatory (1Co 14:26ff). Because public speaking is a great fear for many, participatory meetings are best suited to smaller gatherings of people who know and love one another. After the church meetings in the atriums of Roman villas were replaced by meetings in much larger basilicas, participatory worship was replaced with scripted, stage-like performances by professionals. The practical reality of the priesthood of the believer was lost until the Reformation.

Communion Community

The Lord's Supper was originally celebrated weekly as an actual meal (the *Agapé* feast, 1Co 11). Each local church should be like a family. One of the most common things that families do is to eat together. The larger the congregation, the less family-like, and more impersonal, will be the Lord's Supper as an actual meal. Early church meetings,

---

[15] Robert Banks, *Paul's Idea of Community: The Early House Churches in Their Historical Setting* (Grand Rapids: Eerdmans, 1988), 41–42.

[16] There are more than fifty of these commands, such as love one another, give preference to one another, encourage one another, agree with one another, accept one another, and submit to one another.

centered around the Lord's Table, were times of great fellowship, community, and encouragement. Rather than being observed in a funereal atmosphere, the Lord's Supper was joyfully celebrated in anticipation of the Wedding Banquet of the Lamb.

Congregational Consensus

Each New Testament church had a plurality of clearly identified leaders who led more by example and persuasion rather than command. Building consensus among the members of the congregation was an important part of the decision-making process. Consensus can be achieved in a church in which everyone knows one another, loves one another, bears with one another, is patient with one another, and is committed to one another. A smaller, informal setting is an effective place for building consensus. However, the larger the fellowship, the more difficult it is to maintain relationships and lines of communication. Intimacy suffers. The church leader becomes inaccessible and will necessarily function like a corporate chief executive officer.

Multiplication

Small churches have great potential for growth through multiplication. New churches grow faster than older ones.[17] New leaders should be continually trained to go out to start new churches. We need to think small in a really big way. Rather than growing a single church ever bigger, we should consider sending clusters of people out to start other churches. We should commit to being a small church that starts other small churches that start yet other small churches.

Resource Allocation

The Director of Missions for the San Antonio Baptist Association, Charles Price, lamented that the typical cost of starting a new church

---

[17] "Why Do Newly Planted Churches Grow Faster than Older Churches?" rmdc.org, accessed September 1, 2016.

in North America was an astounding two million dollars.[18] Jim Henry, pastor of First Baptist Church of Orlando stated: "Our two church plants are going to cost us about $2,450,000 over a three-year period."[19] In light of these staggering figures, we must be creative in finding cost-effective meeting places as our small churches start new small churches. Options include renting an apartment clubhouse, dance academy, storefront, school cafeteria, or community center. Older, kingdom-minded congregations may be willing to let others use their buildings after their services are over. The possibility of meeting in someone's home under the right circumstances should not be ruled out. It can still be a viable option: perhaps, the best one. A suitable home would have a large gathering area and ample off-street parking (a problem first-century house churches did not have to deal with). Some homeowners have built what appears to be a four-car garage behind their home for the church to meet in.

Disciple Making

Are you effectively making disciples? One of the first mega-church leaders frankly admitted that although the church attracted over 20,000 attendees weekly, it was not making disciples. They decided to "take out a clean sheet of paper and we rethink all of our old assumptions."[20] We would argue that disciples are best made in the context of the close relationships of small churches.

Proportions
Scores, Not Hundreds

Because first-century churches met almost exclusively in private homes, the typical congregation of the apostolic era was relatively

---

18   Email exchange with author, May 8, 2013.

19   "How Much Does It Cost to Start a Church?" MissionalChallenge.com, accessed September 1, 2016.

20   Bob Burney, "Seeker Friendly Church Leader Admits They Have Done It All Wrong." ReformationHarvestFire.com. Accessed 06/22/2023

small.[21] Though house churches were at the opposite end of the spectrum from modern-day megachurches, it is important to avoid the mistake of thinking *too* small. The size should be just right: not too big and not too small (neither mega nor micro). There were no more people than would fit in a wealthy person's home (in the atrium, courtyard, or living area). The Matthew 18 restoration process detailed by Jesus clearly assumes more people than "us four and no more." There was a single house church meeting in Corinth; counting the people using their spiritual gifts in 1 Corinthians 14 reveals a surprising number of believers. Early house churches were able to support qualified widows and elders. This would have required more than just a handful of believers (1Ti 5:3–16). Having a plurality of elders in a church is unlikely in a setting that is too small (Acts 14:23). The early churches meeting in Roman villas typically consisted of scores of people, not hundreds and certainly not thousands.[22]

Roman Villas

As previously noted, Scripture indicates that early churches met in the homes of their wealthier members. This may have been because of the larger size of the homes and the hosts' ability to provide much of the food for the love feasts. The challenge in worshiping in a home today is that the largest room in modern homes is often far smaller than the largest room in first-century Roman villas. They were big, semipublic houses. Rooms facing the street were often businesses. A hallway between them led into the atrium, at the far end of which was the business office. It was not unusual for strangers to be in and out of a home. In addition, multiple generations of a family typically dwelled under the same roof. There were large areas, such as the atrium, in

---

[21] While it cannot be said with certainty that every church met in a home, it is a fact that when a meeting place is specified in Scripture, it is in a home. Perhaps some congregations met in larger buildings; however, this argument is based on assumptions.

[22] The Jerusalem Church had thousands of members who meet at various houses (Acts 5:42). The short-lived, large meetings in the temple were special ministry meetings rather than regular church meetings.

which the church could gather. Beyond the business office was an even larger semi-covered enclosed courtyard. Spacious living rooms were often built around the courtyard. Enough believers were able to gather for a variety of spiritual gifts to be manifested, for multiple people to be present who had the same gift, for there to be a plurality of elders, and for qualified pastor-teachers to be financially supported. (The pastor-teachers were thus free to devote themselves to disciple-making, in-depth teaching, and leadership).

Archaeology

The meeting room of the Lullingstone Villa house church in Kent, England (built during the Roman occupation) was approximately 15 feet by 21 feet.[23] By modern standards, this would seat approximately 50 people.[24] William Smith's 19th century study of Pompeii revealed that the atrium in the Roman villa of the "tragic poet" measured 20 feet by 28 feet.[25] This would have seated 60 to 80 people. The *ESV Study Bible* notes that early Christian churches "met in homes.... There is extensive archaeological evidence from many cites showing that some homes were structurally modified to hold such churches."[26] One such modified home that was known to host a church was found in Dura-Europos in modern Syria. According to the archaeologists who excavated it, it could seat 65 to 70 people.[27] Since early believers had more of an Asian mindset about personal space, it may have seated more than 70 people. Jerome Murphy-O'Connor compared six Roman-era villas and found the average atrium size to be nearly 800 square feet.[28] Allowing 6 square

---

[23] "Lullingstone Roman Villa," English-Heritage.org.uk. Measurements taken from schematic.

[24] "Space Calculator for Banquet & Meeting Rooms," BanquetTablesPro.com, accessed October 4, 2016.

[25] William Smith, *Dictionary of Greek and Roman Antiquities* (London: John Murray, 1875), 430.

[26] Dennis, *ESV Study*, 2217.

[27] Synder, *Church Life*, 70. The impluvium was tiled, and benches were added around the walls. In addition, a wall between adjoining rooms was removed, thus creating a 714-square-foot area. A raised area was added at the front. Whether this was for a podium is unclear.

[28] Jerome Murphy-O'Connor, *Saint Paul's Corinth: Texts and Archaeology* (Collegeville: Liturgical Press, 2002), 180.

feet per person, this could accommodate approximately 130 people. Luke recorded that 120 believers were assembled in the upper room of a house (Acts 1:13, 15, 2:1–2).

The Rule of 150

In *The Tipping Point*, Malcolm Gladwell quoted British anthropologist Robin Dunbar on the Rule of 150: "The figure of 150 seems to represent the maximum number of individuals with whom we can have a genuinely social relationship, the kind of relationship that goes with knowing who they are and how they relate to us."[29] Dunbar noted, for example, that military units are typically kept at fewer than 150 because "orders can be implemented and unruly behavior controlled on the basis of personal loyalties and direct man-to-man contacts."[30] Another example cited was the Hutterites, Anabaptist communalists, who for hundreds of years have had a strict policy of splitting a colony into two when it approaches 150 people. The Hutterites discovered that with a greater number, people became divided and alienated. Hutterite leader Bill Gross opined: "Keeping things under 150 just seems to be the best and most efficient way to manage a group of people.... When things get larger than that, people become strangers to one another." He said that as a colony approaches 150, "You get two or three groups within the larger group. That is something you really try to prevent, and when it happens it is a good time to branch out."[31] Gladwell concluded: "The size of a group is another one of those subtle contextual factors that can make a big difference.... Crossing the 150 line is a small change that can make a big difference."[32]

Multiplication

When first-century congregations grew, they obviously did not

---

[29]   Malcom Gladwell, *The Tipping Point* (New York: Little, Brown and Company, 2002), 179.

[30]   Ibid., 180, 182, 186.

[31]   Ibid., 181.

[32]   Ibid., 182–183.

erect ever-bigger buildings. Instead, they multiplied, continually training leaders and sending out subgroups to plant new churches. Following this approach, rather than growing a congregation ever larger, our goal should be to start new small churches that start other small churches.[33] Small churches align very much with the size of the apostolic churches that met in Roman villas.

Perspective
Relational Strengths

Small churches have both advantages and disadvantages. They can play to their relational strengths by incorporating various ancient church growth strategies (see previous chapters). According to the Barna Group's research, people younger than 35 years are the most likely group to consider attending a small church. Their desire is to be known and to feel connected. This can be more difficult to achieve in larger churches. On the other hand, people with children were often looking for a church that offers an impressive children's ministry. Such programs require funding for first-class facilities and the hiring of competent staff. This would be financially difficult for smaller churches.[34] However, most small churches do not follow the previously mentioned growth strategies of the ancient church. The adoption of these strategies makes a big difference in attracting and retaining people.

Reproduction

Leading a small church to adopt early church practices will result in blessing. It will foster spiritual growth. It will likely create a contagious excitement that will lead to numerical growth. The temptation is to enjoy this growth, allowing the original church to become much bigger than a typical church in the apostolic era. Instead of pursuing the

---

[33] Wilson & Ferguson, *Becoming a Level Five Multiplying Church Field Guide* (Exponential Resources, 2015).

[34] "Small Churches Struggle to Grow Because of the People They Attract," Barna.org, accessed September 01, 2016.

continual growth of a single congregation, maintaining the New Testament example of multiplying Roman villa-sized churches should be the goal. Reproduction should be built into the church's DNA. There is a need to continually teach the men to be leaders in their homes and the church. New leaders from within should be trained. Once the leadership is in place, a sizable portion of the original church should be sent out to start another small church.

Practicum

Strategically Small

Megachurch pastor Adrian Rogers joked to those in his congregation who preferred a smaller church: "Just sit in one of the first ten rows and don't look back!"[35] However, a genuine advantage for small churches lies in being positioned to reap strategic benefits from adopting the small-church growth strategies of the ancient church. This includes participatory worship, the weekly Lord's Supper/*Agapé*), a plurality of co-equal elders who lead with the servant love of Christ, a commitment to congregational consensus, and an understanding of the vital importance of making disciples by regularly teaching people to observe all that Jesus commanded. Small churches that follow the ways of the early church are in a good position to offer what many are looking for: genuine fellowship, lasting and transparent relationships, and less politics.

Church Houses

A church house is not the church; it is just a sheep shed. Thus, Donald Guthrie concluded: "The expression 'in church' (en *ekklésia*) ... refers to an assembly of believers. There is no suggestion of a special building. Indeed, the idea of a church as representing a building is totally alien to the NT."[36] It is interesting that the New Testament is devoid of any instructions for the construction of special buildings for

---

[35] Rogers, *Adrianisms*, 266.

[36] Guthrie, *Theology*, 744.

worship. This is far different from Mosaic legislation, which contained exacting blueprints for the tabernacle. When the New Covenant writers broached this subject, they pointed out that the believers themselves are the temple of the Holy Spirit: living stones that come together to constitute a spiritual house with Jesus Christ as the Chief Cornerstone (1Pe 2:4–5; Eph 2:19–22; 1Co 3:16, 6:19). Itinerant English Bible teacher Arthur Wallis said: "In the Old Testament, God had a sanctuary for His people; in the New, God has His people as a sanctuary."[37] Southern Baptist pastor John Havlik offered these penetrating words: "The church is never a place, but always a people; never a fold but always a flock; never a sacred building but always a believing assembly. The church is you who pray, not where you pray. A structure of brick or marble can no more be the church than your clothes of serge or satin can be you. There is in this world ... no sanctuary of man but the soul."[38]

Some Christians place too much emphasis on church buildings. Bernard of Clairvaux wrote: "I will not dwell upon the vast height of their churches, their unconscionable length, their preposterous breadth, their richly polished paneling, all of which distracts the eyes of the worshipper and hinders his devotion. You throw money into your decorations ... your candlesticks as tall as trees, great masses of bronze of exquisite workmanship, and as dazzling with their precious stones as the lights that surmount them, what, think you, is the purpose of all this? Will it melt a sinner's heart and not rather keep him gazing in wonder? O vanity of vanities—no, insanity rather than vanity!"[39]

Due diligence is needed before spending exorbitant amounts acquiring church buildings that will sit empty most of the week. This is money that might be better spent on disciple-making, evangelism, benevolence, or support for local church leaders and missionaries. Charles Spurgeon asked: "Does God need a house? He who made the heavens

---

[37] Arthur Wallis, *The Radical Christian* (Rancho Cordova, CA: City Hill Publishing, 1987).

[38] John Havlik, *People-Centered Evangelism* (Nashville: Broadman, 1971), 47.

[39] David Knowles, *The Monastic Orders in England* (Cambridge: Cambridge University Press, 1950), 82.

and the earth, does he dwell in temples made with hands? What crass ignorance this is! No house beneath the sky is more holy than the place where a Christian lives, and eats, and drinks, and sleeps, and praises the Lord in all that he does, and there is no worship more heavenly than that which is presented by holy families, devoted to the fear of the Lord."[40] The real issue is, thus, not where a church meets, but where and how it can best do what God requires of it.

House Churches

Under the right circumstances, a private home can be the ideal setting for a church meeting. J. Vernon McGee predicted: "As the church started in the home, it is going to come back to the home."[41] The smaller, homey setting fosters genuine friendships. The celebration of the Lord's Supper as a fellowship meal in this relaxed, unhurried, comfortable setting helps to build unity and love. A home is not big enough to accommodate a huge number of people. Thus, participatory worship in which each person contributes according to his spiritual gifts is much more intimate and meaningful. Meeting in a suitable private dwelling is a good use of scarce financial resources. Every member's participation and ministry were highly valued and encouraged in the early church. Thus, a large home is still a setting in which every person can comfortably contribute and function for the edification of the whole body of Christ. House churches can be simple, wonderful, down-to-earth (yet touching heaven) expressions of new covenant church life. Another advantage of a church that meets in a home is that the money that would normally have gone toward rent can be used to support a church leader (though he would likely still need to be bi-vocational).

Houston Baptist University professor Peter Davids and German Baptist pastor Siegfried Grossmann offered this studied insight: "The witness of the New Testament is clear: the living space of the church

---

40   Charles Spurgeon, sermon, "Building the Church," April 5, 1874.

41   J. Vernon McGee, *Thru the Bible: Philippians and Colossians* (Nashville: Thomas Nelson, 1991), 190.

was the house. We judge the church-historical development to be a step backward from relationship to religion. Today, a new desire for a face-to-face fellowship has broken out. For too long we have exclusively seen the formal church services as the center of the church and neglected our concrete life together in houses. We cannot slavishly imitate what took place earlier, but we should be challenged anew by this foundational structure of the church as a network of house churches. We see the following concrete challenges: The church needs face-to-face fellowship. The church dare not bracket out daily life from the life of the church. The church needs structures through which the reality of concrete life can be encouraged. The church must keep in balance the handing out of the word and the handing out of life."[42]

Many modern homes are too small to hold enough believers to have the strength of a first-century Roman villa-sized house church. In a typical modern Western house church, no one is qualified to serve as an elder. In addition, no one has the free time to consistently devote to in-depth teaching. The reproduction of new house churches will be hindered because of the critical shortage of qualified leaders (the Holy Spirit did not gift enough leaders for so many sub-biblical micro churches). Lacking both qualified leadership and in-depth teaching, the house church becomes somewhat of a "bless me" club. The fellowship of the *Agapé* is marvelous, the worship is wonderful, and the children have a good time playing together. However, no significant discipleship occurs. Outreach is minimal. Thus, it is important to avoid the mistake of thinking too small. Even if the home is big enough to host scores of people, the neighbors will not be pleased if the surrounding streets are choked with traffic every Lord's Day. Many areas have passed zoning ordinances against churches in homes for this reason. This situation is not helped by the fact that house churches are perceived as cultic by many in society. In addition, they are not taken seriously by the typical believer. Maybe worst of all is their tendency to attract an

---

[42]   Davids and Grossmann, "House."

unusually high percentage of "disciples" who are anti-authority and socially dysfunctional, espouse aberrant theologies, or hold secondary issues so dear that they have separated themselves from other believers (factiousness).

In sum, accomplishing what the early church achieved might necessitate not meeting in a home. A dynamic equivalent might be more appropriate. Therefore, the emphasis should be on following the general New Testament principle of smaller churches, not simply meeting in homes. For a church to function as effectively as the early church, the size and layout of the building should be carefully considered. Ideally, the building should feel homey. It should be designed to hold a relatively small congregation, and the seating arrangement should be flexible. Because eating together was a major part of early gatherings, the church should have a food preparation area (e.g., sink, long countertop, refrigerator, etc.) and a dining area. To help families with small children, it should have a nursery area and safe indoor and outdoor play areas. There should be ample parking.

To overcome the limitations of modern Western homes, which are smaller than Roman villas, the elders from the various house churches in an area could meet weekly as a sort of presbytery. A mid-week centralized teaching that is open to all house churches could be offered by church leaders who are especially gifted in teaching. The house congregations could also meet together in a large, rented facility monthly or quarterly for worship and encouragement.

Many forward thinkers suspect that the Western church is on the path to persecution. For example, biblical teachings against homosexuality will be viewed as hate speech. Christians will be painted by the media as close-minded, right-wing bigots who are on the wrong side of history. The tax-exempt status of churches could be revoked by government legislation when sexual freedom trumps religious liberty (the power to tax is the power to destroy). In times of persecution, meeting in private homes is an attractive option.

Bi-Vocational Leaders

Southeastern Baptist Seminary president Danny Aiken opined that as the number of Christians recedes in the West, house churches are the wave of the future. He further advises seminarians to prepare to be bi-vocational.[43] Bi-vocational ministry was the norm in New Testament times. Jesus' statement that it is more blessed to give than to receive is famous; however, the context is much less known. These words do not appear in any of the four Gospels. They were cited by Paul at a church leader's conference. Paul assumed that most of the leaders would earn their living from regular jobs, just as he did. Thus, they would be the givers of silver and gold to the church rather than the recipients: "I coveted no one's silver or gold or apparel. You yourselves know that these hands ministered to my necessities and to those who were with me. In all things I have shown you that by working hard in this way we must help the weak and remember the words of the Lord Jesus, how he himself said, 'It is more blessed to give than to receive'" (Acts 20:33–35).

Church leaders feel a great burden to make disciples. They identify with Jeremiah, who said: "If I say, 'I will not mention him, or speak any more in his name,' there is in my heart as it were a burning fire shut up in my bones, and I am weary with holding it in, and I cannot" (Jer 20:9). This burden creates the tension expressed by a bi-vocational leader who wrote: "I leave home at 5:30 a.m. and return at 5:30 p.m. While I see the people around me as an open field for ministry, so much of my time is consumed in commercial activities that I feel like there is something beyond all this that pulls my mind to it perpetually."[44] Perhaps solace can be found in Paul's example. He was God's premier evangelist, church planter, and disciple maker. Yet God, in his sovereignty, felt that making tents was a good use of Paul's time. In His divine wisdom, God also judged that it would be better for Paul to spend

---

43 Personal conversation with author at Feed My Sheep conference, Atlanta, May 9, 2014.

44 Email correspondence between author and South African church leader Chad Hutchinson.

much of his time in jail, unable to do the "Lord's work." However, were it not for Paul's time in jail, the church might not have his prison epistles. Our idea and God's idea of the Lord's work might be different. None of us knows the work that God is doing in our lives to prepare us for whatever comes next. Are we in the places that He has called us to serve? If so, what else can we do but continue to be faithful and to remain where we are? Jesus promised to build the church. Let us rest in God's sovereignty.

Small in a Big Way

Church leaders deeply desire to see their churches grow spiritually and numerically. They want to reach people with the Gospel and to see lives transformed. A small church with the life of Christ that adopts early church practices will likely grow spiritually and numerically. As people's needs are met as they walk closer with Christ, they become excited and cannot help but tell others about Christ and His church. Growing churches love, and loving churches grow.

The temptation will be to allow a small church to grow ever larger. However, beyond a certain size, a church will begin to lose the small-church advantage. Following the practices of the New Testament will become increasingly difficult. The church will become a victim of its own success. The solution is to intentionally keep the church relatively small through the multiplication of small churches, the ongoing training of new leaders, and the deployment of the best people to start new congregations. The goal is dynamic small churches that start other dynamic small churches that start yet other dynamic small churches.

We must celebrate the multiplication of small churches, and gauge success by multiplication rather than addition. Church growth consultant Bill Easum suggests: "Success shouldn't be measured solely by our worship attendance. Success must also be measured by how many people we send out and release into ministry."[45] There are 400,000 churches in

---

[45] Bill Easum, "Ripples of Multiplication," m.exponential.org, accessed August 31, 2016.

America with an average size of 100.[46] If only ten percent start a new church in the next five years, that would be 40,000 new churches. Now, this is something to get excited about!

Smaller churches have strategic, divinely-designed size advantages for effective ministry: closeness, intimacy, refreshing simplicity, ease of multiplication, one-another ministry, face-to-face fellowship, the Lord's Supper as an *Agapé* meal, less bureaucracy, less management headache, church discipline, meaningful participatory worship, and in achieving consensus. After all: "God chose what is foolish in the world to shame the wise; God chose what is weak in the world to shame the strong; God chose ... even things that are not, to bring to nothing things that are, so that no human being might boast in the presence of God" (1Co 1:27-2).

Discussion Questions

1. What is the evidence that persecution was not the only reason the early church met in homes?

2. Some argue that Roman villa-sized churches were characteristic of the church in its infancy. It was right and natural, they argue, for each church to mature beyond the confines of a home and to build ever larger meeting places. How do you feel about this?

3. Were smaller congregations merely an incidental fact of history, or were they a purposeful part of the blueprint for effective church ministry? Why?

4. Why might the apostles have laid down a purposeful pattern of small churches?

5. What are the practical advantages and disadvantages of meeting in a home?

6. What might be the psychological effects of the size of a congregation on a church meeting and on those in attendance?

7. How would the number of people involved affect a church's ability

---

[46] Bob Roberts, "Multiplication Essentials," m.exponential.org, accessed August 31, 2016.

to have a participatory meeting or to achieve congregational consensus?

8. What advantages for growth and reproduction might house churches have over fellowships that have to build church houses?

9. What should be done in a situation in which a home is too small to host a church meeting?

10. How did New Testament churches grow numerically yet continue to meet in private homes?

NTRF.org has audio, video, articles, and a teacher's discussion guide on small church theology.

Strategy #6

Inspired Traditions For Ministry Success

Why should doing church the first-century way matter to you? The potential achievement of God's purposes for His body awaits your fellowship if you adopt the examples given to us in the New Testament. Jesus did not leave us wondering about the best ecclesiology. Through the apostles, He equipped the first Christians with timeless, New Testament traditions for success in ministry. In view of the unique relationship between Jesus and His apostles, we should take care to not neglect the small-church practices they modeled. They are strategies for success.

Profit

According to Stanley Greenslade, an evangelical professor of church history at Oxford University, "The church exists to promote the worship of God, the inner life of the spirit, the evangelization of the world and the molding of society according to the will of God."[1] Jesus knew the best ways to achieve these purposes. The apostles intentionally modeled these practices for us in the churches they founded. Their example was intended to constitute normal and universal church practice. God gave Israel a clear pattern for the Tabernacle and worship in the Old Covenant. What pattern did He give for worship in the New Covenant? God's spiritual Temple must be built on the Chief Cornerstone both in doctrine and sound practice. Adopting the ways of the Apostles better allows the Spirit to create unity, community, commitment, and love in a body of believers. Growing churches love, and loving churches grow.[2]

Presumption

Church leaders have two options for ecclesiology. One is to adopt the ways of the apostles. The other is to follow a path of their own choosing. Regarding historical precedence, Gordon Fee and Douglas Stuart, in *How to Read the Bible for All It's Worth*, state: "Our assumption, along with many others, is that unless Scripture explicitly tells us we must do something, what is merely narrated or described can never function in a normative way."[3] No one, for example, would advocate following Jephthah's tragic example in Judges 11:29ff. However, when it comes to church practice, Fee and Stuart also noted that "almost all biblical Christians tend to treat precedent as having normative authority to some degree or another."[4] What evidence is there that New Testament traditions for church practice were not "merely" described in Scripture but were intended to function in a normative way?

---

1   Stanley Greenslade, "Early Christian Church", *Encyclopedia Britannica*, 14th ed. (1973), s.v.

2   Adrian Rogers, *Adrianisms* (Collierville: Innovo Press, 2015), 271.

3   Gordon Fee and Douglas Stuart, *How to Read the Bible for All Its Worth*, 2nd ed. (Grand Rapids: Zondervan, 1982), 97.

4   Gordon Fee and Douglas Stuart, *How to Read the Bible for All Its Worth*, 4th ed. (Grand Rapids: Zondervan, 2014), 124.

Proof #1—Holding to Tradition Is Praiseworthy

1 Corinthians 11–14 constitutes a four-chapter section on church practice. In this passage, Paul revealed his attitude about following his ecclesiological traditions: "I commend you because you remember me in everything and maintain the traditions even as I delivered them to you" (1Co 11:2). He praised the church at Corinth for holding to his traditions.

Worship Traditions

The Greek for "traditions," *paradosis*, means "that which is passed on."[5] It differs from the Greek word for "teaching" (*didaché*). In his commentary on 1 Corinthians, Gordon Fee pointed out that in the context of 1 Corinthians 11, *paradosis* specifically refers to religious traditions regarding worship.[6] This same Greek word in verb form is found a few paragraphs later with regard to the practice of the Lord's Supper—that it was "passed on" from Paul to the church (11:23).

Traditions (Plural), Not Tradition

It is significant that the word "traditions" in 1 Corinthians 11:2 is plural. Paul clearly had in mind more than the one tradition dealt with in 1 Corinthians 11a.[7] The words "even as" in 11:2 indicate the degree of their compliance with these traditions: *exactly* as passed on to them. Paul praised the church for holding precisely to his traditions regarding worship. He would likely feel the same about our churches following the traditions he established for church practice.

Paradigmatic Law

Mosaic legislation was paradigmatic in nature. It was case law. Only a few legal examples were recorded by Moses. The Israelites were

---

[5]   Bauer, *Lexicon*, 615.

[6]   Fee, "Corinthians", 499.

[7]   Ibid., 500.

expected to apply these case studies to other areas of life not specifically cited. Similarly, we argue that adherence to apostolic tradition is paradigmatic in nature. If we observe that the apostles were pleased when a church followed one specific tradition of church practice (1 Corinthians 11:2), then we would be expected to apply that approval to other patterns we see modeled by the apostles in their establishment of churches. The church, the Bride of Christ, is too eternally important to allow her to deviate from traditions established by the Lord and His apostles.

Good & Bad Tradition

Of course, not all religious traditions are good. The tradition of the Pharisees undermined God's commands. The same word used by Paul in 1 Corinthians 11:2 was also used by Jesus when He asked the Pharisees, "Why do you break the commandment of God for the sake of your tradition (*paradosis*)?" (Mt 15:3). In contrast, Paul blessed the Corinthians for following his traditions. Apostolic traditions are consistent with the teachings of Christ. Thus, holding to the traditions of the apostles is thus praiseworthy, as seen in Paul's praise for the Corinthian church (11:2).

Proof #2—Holding to Tradition was Expected

The churches of the New Testament were expected to follow apostolic traditions for church practice. In the four-chapter section on church practice referenced above (1Co 11–14), Paul quieted those who disagreed with his traditions by appealing to the universal practice of all the other churches: "If anyone is inclined to be contentious, we have no such practice, nor do the churches of God" (1Co 11:16). This statement was designed to settle any objections. Paul expected all churches to do the same things. Just to realize that one was different was enough to silence opposition. Prior emphasis had obviously been given to certain practices that were *supposed to be done the same way, everywhere.*

This indicates a uniformity of practice in all New Testament churches.

As in All the Churches

In 1 Corinthians 14:33b–35, Paul referred to something else that was true universally: "As in *all the churches* of the saints, the women should keep silent in the churches" (italics mine). Paul again appealed to a universal pattern that existed in all churches as a basis for obedience.[8] The point to be observed is that all churches were expected to follow the same practices in their meetings.

Did the Word of God Come from You?

The Corinthians were tempted to do things differently from other churches. Thus, after detailing how worship services should be conducted, Paul chided them: "Or was it from you that the word of God came? Or are you the only ones it has reached?" (1Co 14:36). The obvious answer to both questions is *no*. These two questions were designed to keep the Corinthians in line with the practice of all the other churches. They had no authority to deviate from the church traditions established by the apostles. Holding to apostolic traditions (New Testament church patterns) was expected in the first century. Perhaps it should be today as well. We should ask ourselves: Did the word of God come from our churches? Are our churches the only ones it has reached? If the Corinthian church had no authority to deviate from the traditions of the apostles, then neither do we.

Proof #3—Holding to Tradition Is Commanded

Although apostolic traditions make for interesting history, many think that following them is optional. What, then, are we to make of 2 Thessalonians 2:15, which actually *commands* us to "stand firm and hold to the traditions"?9 It appears that it is not just apostolic *teachings*

---

8   For help interpreting 1 Corinthians 14:33b-35, see "Women: Silent in Church" at NTRF.org.
9   Imperative mode in Greek.

to which we should adhere, but also apostolic *traditions* (as revealed exclusively within the pages of Scripture).[10]

Traditions

The overall context of 2 Thessalonians 2:15 refers to the apostles' teaching tradition concerning end-time events, not church practice *per se*. However, the word "traditions" (2:15) is yet again plural. The author clearly had more traditions in mind than merely the one teaching tradition about the second coming. Would this command not also apply in principle to his traditions regarding church order, which are modeled in the New Testament? We are to follow the traditions of the apostles, not only in their theology, but also in their practice.

A Tradition of Hard Work

A similar attitude towards tradition is expressed in the next chapter: "Now we command you, brothers, in the name of our Lord Jesus Christ, that you keep away from any brother who is walking in idleness and not in accord with the tradition that you received from us. For you yourselves know how you ought to imitate us...." (2 Th 3:6-7). The word "tradition" here clearly refers to practice more than doctrine. It is clear that the apostles wanted the churches to follow their traditions of *both* theology and practice. Should we limit those apostolic traditions that we follow *only* to work habits?

Proof #4—Holding to Tradition Is Logical

It is logical—it just makes sense—to follow the church practice traditions of the apostles (as recorded in Scripture). If anyone truly understood the purpose of the church, surely it was the apostles. They were handpicked and personally trained by Jesus for three years. After His resurrection, our Lord appeared to them over a forty-day period

---

10   One should distinguish between apostolic tradition, as recorded in the pages of the New Testament, and the later historical tradition of Catholicism and Orthodoxy.

(Acts 1:3). Jesus then sent the Holy Spirit to teach them things He had not taught them (Jn 14–16). Paul received further revelation from Jesus during his fourteen years in the wilderness. The things Jesus taught these men about the church were naturally reflected in the way they set up and organized churches.

A Definite Order

Paul's letter to Titus dealt directly with church practice: "This is why I left you in Crete, so that you might put what remained into order, and appoint elders in every town as I directed you" (Titus 1:5). It is evident from this passage that the apostles had a definite way they wanted things done regarding church practice. It was not left up to each individual assembly to find its own way. There was obviously a definite "order," pattern, or tradition that was followed in organizing the churches. Similarly, in 1 Corinthians 11:34 (another passage about church practice), Paul wrote, "The rest I will *set in order* when I come" (KJV, italics mine). It is logical—it just makes sense—to prefer the church traditions of the apostles. If the apostles were to return and see how modern churches function, would they be pleased or grieved?

Be Imitators of Me

Paul boldly offered himself as an example to be followed with regard to his faithful service to Christ: "I urge you, then, be imitators of me. That is why I sent you Timothy ... to remind you of my ways in Christ, as I teach them everywhere in every church" (1Co 4:16–17). Taking this a step further, for us to imitate Paul's ways in Christ regarding church practice would arguably be a wise choice for any fellowship.

Proof #5—Holding to Tradition Brings God's Peaceful Presence

The church at Philippi was told how to have the God of Peace be with them: "What you have learned and received and heard and seen in me—practice these things, and the God of peace will be with you"

(Php 4:9). The context concerned such practices as imitating Christ's humility, putting others first, and rejoicing in the Lord. By extension, could it not also include the way Paul organized churches? It is clear from Scripture how the Apostles designed churches to function. To by-pass apostolic tradition in this area may, therefore, be to bypass some of God's blessings. Could fellowships that follow apostolic church practice enjoy more of God's peaceful presence?

Professors

Professors Fee and Stuart acknowledge that for many believers, Acts "not only tells us the history of the early church, but it also serves as the normative model for the church of all times."[11] They go on to recognize that large movements and new denominations have been "founded partly on the premise that virtually all New Testament patterns should be restored as fully as possible in modern times."[12]

Teaching by Example

Early Southern Baptist Theologian J. L. Dagg believed that if the apostles "taught us, by example, how to organize and govern churches, we have no right to reject their instruction and captiously insist that nothing but positive command shall bind us. Instead of choosing to walk in a way of our own devising, we should take pleasure to walk in the footsteps of those holy men from whom we have received the word of life.... Respect for the Spirit by which they were led should induce us to prefer their modes of organization and government to such as our inferior wisdom might suggest."[13]

The Form of the New Testament Church

Anglican clergyman Roger Williams believed churches should

---

11   Fee and Stuart, *Worth*, 4th ed., 112.

12   Ibid.,130.

13   J.L. Dagg, *A Treatise on Church Order* (Harrisonburg: Gano Books, 1990), 84.

strive to follow New Testament church forms and ordinances as closely as possible.[14] This belief led Williams to found the Rhode Island colony on the New Testament pattern of a separation between church and state, and in 1638 to plant the first Baptist church in North America.

A Permanent Pattern

According to E.H. Broadbent, church historian and undercover missionary to closed nations, "Events in the history of the churches in the time of the apostles have been selected and recorded in the Book of Acts in such a way as to provide a permanent pattern for the churches. Departure from this pattern has had disastrous consequences, and all revival and restoration have been due to some return to the pattern and principles in the Scriptures."[15]

Our Pattern for All Time

According to Chinese church leader Watchman Nee, "Acts is the 'genesis' of the church's history, and the Church in the time of Paul is the 'genesis' of the Spirit's work.... We must return to 'the beginning.' Only what God has set forth as our example in the beginning is the eternal Will of God. It is the Divine standard and our pattern for all time.... God has revealed His Will, not only by giving orders, but by having certain things done in His church, so that in the ages to come others might simply look at the pattern and know His will."[16]

A Universal Pattern

It was missionary martyr Jim Elliot's firm conviction that "The pivot point hangs on whether God has revealed a universal pattern for the church in the New Testament. If He has not, then anything will do so

---

14 Edwin Gaustad, *Liberty of Conscience: Roger Williams in America* (Grand Rapids: Eerdmans, 1991), 106.

15 E.H. Broadbent, *The Pilgrim Church* (Grand Rapids: Gospel Folio Press, 1999), 26.

16 Watchman Nee, *The Normal Christian Church Life* (Colorado Springs: International Students Press, 1969), 8–9.

long as it works. But I am convinced that nothing so dear to the heart of Christ as His Bride should be left without explicit instructions as to her corporate conduct.... It is incumbent upon me, if God has a pattern for the church, to find and establish that pattern, at all costs."[17]

The Divinely Planned Structure

Pastor and author A.W. Tozer wrote, "The temptation to introduce 'new' things into the work of God has always been too strong for some people to resist. The Church has suffered untold injury at the hands of well-intentioned but misguided persons, who have felt that they know more about running God's work than Christ and His apostles did! A solid train of boxcars would not suffice to haul away the religious truck that has been brought into the service of the Church with the hope of improving on the original pattern. These things have been, one and all, great hindrances to the progress of the Truth, and have so altered the divinely planned structure that the apostles, were they to return to earth today, would scarcely recognize the misshapen thing which has resulted!"[18] He concluded: "If the Holy Spirit was withdrawn from the church today, 95 percent of what we do would go on and no one would know the difference. If the Holy Spirit had been withdrawn from the New Testament church, 95 percent of what they did would stop, and everybody would know the difference."[19]

Proposition

What can be concluded about God's interest in your church adhering to New Testament patterns for church practice? Fee and Stuart offered the general observation that what is merely narrated or described

---

[17]   Elizabeth Elliot, *Shadow of The Almighty: Life and Testimony of Jim Elliot* (San Francisco: Harper & Row, 1989), 138–139.

[18]   James Snyder, *Tozer on Worship and Entertainment* (Camp Hill: Wind Hill Publisher, 1997), chap. 17.

[19]   Robert Crosby, "A.W. Tozer on The Holy Spirit & Today's Church," Patheos.com. Accessed October 16, 2016.

can never function in a normative way. In a later edition of their book, they qualified their position somewhat: "Unless Scripture explicitly tells us we must do something, what is only narrated or described does not function in a normative (i.e., obligatory) way—*unless it can be demonstrated on other grounds that the author intended it to function in this way.*"[20] The purpose of this chapter is to demonstrate that the apostles did indeed intend for churches to follow the patterns they laid down for church practice. Holding to their traditions for church practice, which were universally practiced in first-century churches, brings God's peaceful presence. It is logical, praiseworthy, and even commanded. The question thus is not, *Must we do things the way they were done in the New Testament?* Rather, the question is, *why would we want to do things any other way?*

What are some of these ancient apostolic traditions for church practice? Here is a list of some traditions still practiced, and others long neglected:

1. *Meeting weekly on Sunday, the Lord's Day, in honor of Jesus' resurrection.*
2. *Believer's baptism by immersion.*
3. *The separation of church and state.*
4. *A plurality of co-equal male elders leading every congregation.*
5. *Elder-led congregational consensus.*
6. *Participatory "each one has" church meetings.*
7. *Celebrating the Lord's Supper weekly as a fellowship meal.*
8. *Roman villa-sized churches (neither micro nor mega in size).*

Forsake Modern Traditions!

Most churches follow some of these patterns, but not all. *Why not?* Perhaps it is because little attention is paid in seminary to the role apostolic traditions should play. Perhaps it is because most churches

---

[20] Fee and Stuart, *Worth*, 4th ed., 124.

are firmly entrenched in man-made traditions developed long after the apostolic era. Many church leaders have simply adopted historical traditions inherited from their denomination. Is there not a danger of neglecting the inspired tradition of the apostles for the sake of more modern traditions (Mt 15:1–3)?

Deviating from the New Testament Pattern

We argue for consistency. The burden of explanation ought to fall on those who deviate from the New Testament pattern, not on those who desire to follow it. This consistency is especially important because the apostles evidently intended all churches to follow their traditions just as they were handed down (1Co 11:2). Perhaps these patterns of church practice are part of what gave the early church the dynamic that churches today are sometimes missing.

Perspective

Even though all first-century churches adhered to apostolic practices, they were still far from perfect, as seen in Jesus' warnings to the churches in Revelation. However, adopting the ways of the apostles for church life is a strategic stepping stone to putting a fellowship in a better position to be all Christ wants it to be as His body. These practices will enrich your church, but are not the answer to all its problems. For example, without Christ at the center of things, New Testament church life patterns become legalism and death, a hollow form, an empty shell (Jn 15:5).

A Holy Church

At the end of a very long life of faithful ministry, seminary professor L. Reginald Barnard cautioned that one can have a very scriptural idea of how the early church did things and yet miss the real idea of the church entirely. Barnard opined that even if our church is identical to the apostolic ideal, we would accomplish nothing unless that church was holier by far than the church we started with.[21] Heaven forbid that, at the end, we present a form to God instead of a holy people redeemed by the Gospel.

An Imperfect Church

We must always remember that the church is people, the living body of Christ. Jesus died to sanctify His bride, presenting her to Himself without spot or wrinkle, holy and blameless. There is no perfect church. Yet God will do His perfect work in His imperfect church, for it is His church.

A Divine Design

When a church truly has new spiritual wine, the best church-practice wineskin for that wine is apostolic tradition. The church traditions of the apostles are simple, strategic, and scriptural. The most neglected practices are intentionally smaller congregations, participatory church meetings, celebrating the Lord's Supper weekly as a fellowship meal, and servant leadership that builds congregational consensus. Incorporating these traditions into our churches today can result in tremendous blessing. Such churches have a bright future and tremendous potential if their leaders maintain a focus on disciple-making in the context of dynamic, Spirit-filled early church practice. It is a divine design!

Practicum

Lifelessness

Jesus came that we might have life and have it abundantly (Jn 10:10). Critical to any outworking of church life is first having an inner life to work out. Technically correct church practice without the wine of the Spirit is a hollow shell. It is dry, seasoned wood, all stacked up, with no fire. Jesus is the Vine and we are the branches. Apart from Jesus,

---

[21]   Letter to author, May 15, 1991.

we can do nothing (Jn 15:5). It is folly to give attention to outward perfection while neglecting that which is vital—a daily walk with the risen Lord. Jesus is the reality; apostolic church practice is the application of that reality.

License

A temptation for those who truly possess the inner reality of life in Jesus is to treat its outward expression as a matter of liberty. Having the greater (the wine), they feel that they themselves are competent to decide in lesser matters (the wineskin). They believe they have a license from the Spirit to do whatever they please with the outward form. To be bound by the ways of the apostles is seen as mindless aping. However, Jesus warned that pouring new wine into the wrong wineskin could lead to the loss of the wine (Mt 9:17). Do we really know better than the apostles how to organize churches? With specific reference to church practice, Paul admonished: "If anyone thinks that he is a prophet, or spiritual, he should acknowledge that the things I am writing to you are a command of the Lord" (1Co 14:37).

Legalism

The Roman world is gone forever. There is a big difference between holding to apostolic tradition versus mindlessly copying *everything* seen in the New Testament (wearing togas, writing on parchment, reading by oil lamps, etc.). The key is to focus on New Testament church practice. We must also beware of making patterns out of things that are not patterns in the New Testament. For instance, the Christian communalism of Acts 4 was a one-time event for a single church. It is an option for believers of any age, but it is neither a command nor a Scriptural pattern.

Beware of making patterns out of silence. Some are so convinced that we should follow New Testament patterns that they feel they have no freedom to do anything that was not done by the early church. They believe that if a practice is not found in the New Testament, then we can't do it; it is forbidden. For instance, if the New Testament were silent about using musical instruments, then they must not be used. In response, it must first be pointed out that the absence of a mention of a practice is not proof that the early church did not follow that practice. Second, this negative approach is essentially a form of legalism and leads easily to a judgmental spirit. Instead of seeking to positively follow clear New Testament patterns, advocates of this negative hermeneutic are best known for all the things they are against. If it is wrong to practice what the New Testament is silent about, then why did Jesus participate in the festival of Hanukkah and the synagogue system, both of which were extra-biblical, inter-testament historical developments?

Liberty

We advocate a normative hermeneutic: the church should normally hold to apostolic practices followed by the early church. Matters of silence are matters of freedom. If the Bible is silent about something—if there is neither command nor pattern to follow—then we have the liberty to do whatever suits us (following the lead of the Holy Spirit).

Are there ever any good reasons for going against New Testament patterns? Moses told the Israelites to observe a Saturday Sabbath—violating it was a capital offense. However, if an ox fell in the ditch, then work on the Sabbath was permissible. Jesus—the Lord of the Sabbath—clarified that it was also always appropriate to do good works on the Sabbath. He further taught that the Sabbath was made for man and not man for the Sabbath. So, too, the traditions found in the New Testament are there for the sake of the church, not *vice versa*. Scripture indicates that we are generally to hold to the patterns laid down by the apostles. However, there are times when extenuating circumstances argue against keeping some patterns. Just don't let the exception become the rule.

Doing church the New Testament way—as opposed to any other

way—is in the same category as infant baptism versus believer's baptism. Sincere believers disagree over it. One position is in error, but it is a sincere error, and surely not in the same category as lying, stealing, adultery, etc. We have not intended to imply that not doing things the New Testament way is a sin. That said, we do intend to give pause to those not doing things the New Testament way, since the word "command" is used in reference to participatory meetings (1Co 14:37), and since holding to apostolic traditions is also commanded (2Th 2:13). Jesus and the Apostles must have had good reason to set up things the way they did. What potential blessings is your church missing by not following their traditions?

Discussion Questions

1. How can the axiom *form follows function* be applied to how the apostles set up churches?

2. What in the New Testament indicates whether there was a basic uniformity of practice in all early churches?

3. Jesus criticized the Pharisees for holding to Jewish traditions (Mt 15). Paul praised the Corinthians for holding to his traditions (1Co 11). Why the difference?

4. Why is it important to make a distinction between apostolic traditions found in the New Testament and later historical traditions?

5. Mosaic Law was paradigmatic in nature. How would the paradigmatic principle apply to commands in the New Testament to follow specific apostolic traditions (2Th 2:15, 3:6)?

6. What gave the apostles authority to establish patterns that all churches are obliged to follow?

7. What is the difference between holding to apostolic traditions versus mindlessly copying everything seen in the New Testament (wearing sandals, writing on parchment, studying by oil lamps, dressing in togas, etc.)?

8. Jesus washed His disciples' feet. The Jerusalem church practiced communalism. How can we determine what is and is not intended to be an apostolic tradition?

9. What should we make of the fact that there is scholarly consensus regarding the actual practice of the early church in the New Testament?

10. Some think it foolish to try to recreate the primitive church, because it was far from perfect; God expected His church to mature, to grow up, beyond the infancy stage. How would you respond to this argument?

NTRF.org has audio, video, articles, and a teacher's guide on the advantages of holding to timeless New Testament traditions for church practice.

About the Author

Stephen E. Atkerson (M.Div., Mid-America Baptist Seminary) helps bi-vocational and small-church leaders discover shepherding strategies given by Jesus to the early church. He serves as one of the bi-vocational pastors of a small Baptist church he planted in 1991, and for over 30 years has worked with evangelists, missionaries, church planters, and pastors in Asia, the Americas, Europe, and Africa. He is president of the New Testament Reformation Fellowship (NTRF.org), which is dedicated to **helping small churches have a big impact.**

About NTRF.org

The New Testament Reformation Fellowship is a teaching fellowship of pastors helping other church leaders understand how to recapture the intimacy, simplicity, and dynamics of first-century church life. Frankly, we are not smart enough to dream up trendy new ways of doing church. However, we are smart enough to realize that, at least for us, it is best to stick with the tried-and-true examples left by the Twelve. You'll find free video, audio, and columns at NTRF.org. We are also available for consultations with other leaders (take advantage of our 30+ years of doing church this way!).

The essential tenets of the faith to which we subscribe are identical to those found in the doctrinal statement of any sound evangelical institution. Our favorite statement of faith is the *First London Baptist Confession of 1644.*

Bibliography

ADEA. "Critical Thinking Skills Toolkit", ADEA.org. Accessed 2023.

Aristotle. *Aristotle's Rhetoric*, Book I, chapter 2.

Atkerson, Sandra. "Hints for Hosting the Lord's Supper," NTRF.org, 2007.

Banks, Robert. *Paul's Idea of Community: The Early House Churches in Their Historical Setting*, Grand Rapids: Eerdmans, 1988.

Balz, Horst & Schneider, Gerhard, eds. *Exegetical Dictionary of the New Testament*, Vol. 3, Grand Rapids: Eerdmans, 1993.

Barclay, William. "The Letters to the Corinthians," *Daily Study Bible*, Philadelphia: Westminster, 1977.

Barna. "Small Churches Struggle to Grow Because of the People They Attract," Barna.org, 2003.

Barrett, C. K. "Fist Epistle to the Corinthians," *Black's New Testament Commentary*, Peabody: Hendrickson, 1968.

Bartels, K.H., "Remember," *New International Dictionary of New Testament Theology*, Vol. III, ed., Colin Brown, Grand Rapids: Zondervan, 1981.

Bauer, Arndt, Gingrich, Danker. *Greek-English Lexicon of the New Testament*, Chicago: University of Chicago Press, 1979.

Becker, U. & Muller, D. "Proclamation, Preach, Kerygma", *New International Dictionary of New Testament Theology,* Colin Brown, ed., Vol. 3. Grand Rapids: Zondervan, 1978.

Broadbent, E.H. *The Pilgrim Church*, Grand Rapids: Gospel Folio Press, 1999.

Brown, Colin. *New International Dictionary of New Testament Theology*, Grand Rapids: Zondervan, 1981.

Bruce, F.F. "The Book of Acts", *New International Commentary on the New Testament*, Grand Rapids: Eerdmans, 1981.

Burney, Bob. "Seeker Friendly Church Leader Admits They Have Done It All Wrong." ReformationHarvestFire.com. Accessed 2023

Carson, D.A. ed., *Worship by the Book*, Grand Rapids: Zondervan, 2010.

Chesterton, G.K. "Tradition Is the Democracy of the Dead," Chesterton.org.

Coenen, Lothan. "Church," *New International Dictionary of New Testament Theology*, ed., Brown, Colin, Grand Rapids: Zondervan, 1971.

Coverdale, Miles & Knox, John, directors. *1599 Geneva Bible.* White Hall, WV: Telle Lege Press, 2006.

Crosby, Robert. "A.W. Tozer on The Holy Spirit & Today's Church," Patheos.com.

Dagg, J.L. *Manual of Theology: A Treatise on Church Order*, Harrisonburg: Gano Books, 1990.

Davids, Peter & Grossmann, Siegfried. "The Church in the House," paper, 1982.

DeBrès, Gudio. *Belgic Confession.* crcna.org, 1651.

Deddens, Karl. *Where Everything Points to Him*, translated by Theodore Plantinga, Neerlandia: Inheritance Publications, 1993.

Dennis, Lane, & Grudem, Wayne, eds. *ESV Study Bible*, Wheaton: Crossway, 2008.

DeVries, David. "How Much Does It Cost To Start A Church?" MissionalChallenge.com.

DeYoung, Kevin. *Just Do Something* (Chicago: Moody, 2009), 53.

Drane, John. *Introducing the New Testament*, Oxford: Lion, 1999.

Easum, Bill. "Ripples of Multiplication," m.exponential.org, 2016.

Elliot, Elizabeth. *Shadow of the Almighty: Life and Testimony of Jim Elliot*, San Francisco: Harper & Row, 1989.

Ennis, Robert. "Critical thinking and subject specificity: clarification and needed research", Educ Researcher 1989; 18: 4-10.

Fee, Gordon & Stuart, Douglas. *How To Read The Bible For All Its Worth*, 2nd ed., Grand Rapids: Zondervan, 1982.

Fee, Gordon & Stuart, Douglas. *How To Read The Bible For All Its Worth*, 4th ed., Grand Rapids: Zondervan, 2014.

Fee, Gordon. "First Epistle to the Corinthians," *New International Commentary on the New Testament*, Grand Rapids: Eerdmans, 1987.

Ferguson & Wilson, *Becoming a Level Five Multiplying Church Field Guide.* Exponential Resources, 2015.

Gaustad, Edwin. *Liberty of Conscience: Roger Williams In America*, Grand Rapids: Eerdmans, 1991.

Gladwell, Malcom. *The Tipping Point*, New York: Little, Brown and Company, 2002

Gooch, John. *Christian History & Biography*, Issue 37, Carol Stream: Christianity Today, 1993.

Greensdale, Stanley Lawrence. "Early Christian Church," *Encyclopaedia Britannica*, Vol. 7, ed. Warren Preece, Chicago: William Benton, Publisher, 1973.

Grogan, G. W. "Love Feast," *New Bible Dictionary*, ed., J. D. Douglas, Wheaton: Tyndale, 1982.

Grudem, Wayne. "The Nature of Divine Eternity, A Response to William Craig," WayneGrudem.com, 1997.

Guthrie, Donald. *New Testament Theology*, Downers Grove: InterVarsity, 1981.

Hatch, Edwin *The Influence of Greek Ideas and Usages Upon the Christian Church*. Edinburgh: Williams and Norgate, 1891.

Havlik, John. *People Centered Evangelism*, Nashville: Broadman, 1971.

Hendriksen, William. "Exposition of Paul's Epistle to the Romans," *New Testament Commentary*. Grand Rapids: Baker, 1980.

Horne, H.H. *Jesus the Master Teacher.* New York: Association Press, 1920.

Jeremias, Joachim. *The Eucharistic Words of Jesus*, New York: Charles Scribner's Sons, 1966.

John Gooch. *Christian History & Biography*, Issue 37, Carol Stream: Christianity Today, 1993.

Kirby, G.W. *Zondervan Pictorial Encyclopedia of the Bible*, Vol. 1, ed. Merrill C. Tenney, Grand Rapids: Zondervan, 1982.

Knowles, David. *The Monastic Orders in England*, Cambridge: Cambridge University Press, 1950.

Koyzis, David. "The Lord's Supper: How Often?" ReformedWorship.org, 1990.

Lenski, R.C.H. *Interpretation of I and II Corinthians*, Minneapolis: Augsburg, 1943.

Lenski, R.C.H. *Interpretation of the Epistle to the Hebrews and the Epistle of James*, Minneapolis: Augsburg Publishing, 1943.

Mamula, Greg, "Early Christian Table Fellowship Becomes Eucharistic Rite," paper, 2015.

Martin, R. P., "The Lord's Supper," *New Bible Dictionary*, ed. J. D. Douglas, Wheaton: Tyndale, 1982.

Mathison, Keith. *The Shape of Sola Scriptura*, Moscow: Canon Press, 2001.

McGee, J. Vernon. *Thru the Bible: Philippians and Colossians*, Nashville: Thomas Nelson, 1991.

McReynolds, Paul. *Word Study Greek-English New Testament*, Wheaton: Tyndale, 1999.

Milikin, Jimmy. "Disorder Concerning Public Worship," *Mid America Baptist Theological Journal*, Memphis: Mid-America Baptist Seminary Press, 1983.

Mounce, R.H. "Preaching", *New Bible Dictionary*, 2nd edition, JD Douglas, ed., Wheaton: Tyndale, 1982.

Murphy-O'Connor, Jerome. *Saint Paul's Corinth: Texts and Archaeology*, Collegeville: Liturgical Press, 2002.

Nee, Watchman. *The Normal Christian Church Life*, Colorado Springs: International Students Press, 1969.

Norrington, David C. *To Preach or Not to Preach?* Omaha: Ekklesia Press, 1996.

Oyler, Douglas & Romanelli, Frank. "The Fact of Ignorance: Revisiting the Socratic Method as a Tool for Teaching Critical Thinking." ncbi.nlm.nih.gov. 2023.

Pelikan, Jaroslav. "Eucharist," *Encyclopaedia Britannica*, ed. Warren Preece, Vol. 8, Chicago: William Benton, Publisher, 1973.

Platt, David. "How Should We Be Making Disciples?" Radical.net. Accessed 2023.

Turner, Harold *From Temple to Meeting House.* New York: Mouton Publishers, 1979.

Reinecker, Fritz & Rogers, Cleon. *Linguistic Key to the Greek New Testament*, Grand Rapids: Zondervan, 1980.

Ridderbos, Herman. *Paul: An Outline of His Theology*, translated by John R. deWitt, Grand Rapids: Eerdmans, 1975.

Roberts, Bob. "Multiplication Essentials," m.exponential.org, 2016.

Robertson, Archibald & Plummer, Alfred. "1 Corinthians," *International Critical Commentary on the Holy Scriptures of the Old and New Testaments*, New York: Charles Scribner's Sons, 1911.

Rogers, Adrian. *Adrianisms*, Memphis: Innovo Publishing, 2015.

Rogers, Adrian. Revision chairman, *Baptist Faith and Message*, sbc.net, 2000.

Scott, Ernest. *The Nature of the Early Church*, New York, Charles Scribner's Sons, 1941.

Schreiner, Thomas. *Spiritual Gifts: What They Are & Why They Matter.* Nashville: B&H Publishing, 2018.

Schumacher, E.F. "Small is Beautiful," *The Radical Humanist*, Vol. 37, No. 5, August 1973.

Sefton, Henry. *A Lion Handbook—The History of Christianity*, Oxford: Lion, 1988.

Selman, Martin. "House", *New Bible Dictionary*, ed. J. D. Douglas, Wheaton: Tyndale, 1982.

Sider, Ronald. *Rich Christians in an Age of Hunger*, Downers Grove: Intervarsity, 1977.

Scott, Ernest, *The Nature of the Early Church*, New York: Charles Scribner's Sons, 1941.

Smith, William. *Dictionary of Greek and Roman Antiquities*, London: John Murray, 1875.

Snyder, Graydon. *Church Life Before Constantine*, Macon: Mercer University Press, 1991.

Snyder, James. *Tozer on Worship And Entertainment*, Camp Hill: Wind Hill Publisher, 1997.

Spurgeon, Charles. "A Pastoral Visit," ccel.org.

Svendsen, Eric. *The Table of the Lord*, Atlanta: New Testament Reformation Fellowship, 1997.

Thayer, Joseph. *Greek-English Lexicon of the New Testament*, Grand Rapids: Baker, 1977.

Theissen, Gerd. *The Social Setting of Pauline Christianity: Essays on Corinth*, Eugene, OR: Wipf & Stock, 1982.

Thomas, W.H. Griffith. *St. Paul's Epistle to the Romans*, Grand Rapids: Eerdmans, 1984.

Yale University. "Unearthing the Christian Building", *Dura-Europos: Excavating Antiquity*, Yale University Art Gallery.

Vaters, Karl. "The Astonishing Power of Small Churches: Over One Billion Served," ChristianityToday.com, 2016.

Vine, W.E. *Expository Dictionary of New Testament Words*, Iowa Falls: Riverside Book and Bible House, 1952.

von Campenhausen, Hans. *Ecclesiastical Authority and Spiritual Power in the Church of the First Three Centuries.* Stanford: Stanford University Press, 1969.

Wallis, Arthur. *The Radical Christian*, Rancho Cordova: City Hill Publishing, 1987.

Walker, Williston. *History of the Christian Church*, New York: Charles Scribner's Sons, 1970.

Watson, David. *I Believe in the Church*, Great Britain: Hodder & Stoughton, 1978.

Good News

My mother passed away from cancer when I was in high school. I wondered: *What had become of her? Where had she gone? Would I ever see her again?* After much inquiry about life after death, I learned that no matter how good a person was, it would not be good enough to earn heaven. God is so holy that just one sin is all it takes to separate someone from Him. That was bad news. The good news is that Jesus, who is God in human form, died on the cross in order to pay for sin. Since He is infinite God, Jesus was able to suffer in a finite amount of time on the cross what it would take a mere human, who is finite, an infinity of time to suffer in hell. After His death, Jesus literally, bodily rose from the dead on the third day. He conquered death! He then ascended to heaven and from there Christians await his return. Here is a summary of the good news:

God—God is the creator of all things (Ge 1:1). He is perfect, worthy of all worship, has authority over us, and will punish sin (1Jn 1:5, Re 4:11, Ro 2:5-8).

Man—All have sinned and fall short of God's holiness (Ge 1:26-28, Ps 51:5, Ro 3:23). Our sin alienates us from God, and subjects us to His wrath (Ep 2:1-3).

Jesus—Jesus, who is fully God and fully man, lived a sinless life, died on the cross to bear God's wrath in the place of all who would believe in him, and rose from the grave in order to give eternal life to those who believe (Jn 1:1, 1Ti 2:5, Heb. 7:26, Ro 3:21-26, 2Co 5:21, 1Co 15:20-22).

Response—God calls everyone to repent of their sins and trust in Jesus so as to be saved from sin and wrath (Mk 1:15, Acts 20:21, Ro 10:9-10).

Although I had heard of Jesus from earliest memory, my belief in him was not unlike my belief in Albert Einstein: I believed both existed, but did not look to either to do anything for me. I mistakenly thought heaven to be my destiny simply because I sincerely tried to be a good person. However, I discovered that obtaining eternal life is not based on how good I was, but solely on the goodness of Jesus. When I finally realized the truth, I consciously transferred trust for my eternal destiny from me, and anything good in me, over to Jesus. I confessed the same thing that Thomas, an early believer, confessed: "My Lord and my God!" (John 20:28). After trusting in Jesus, he gave me a desire to obey His teachings: "If you love me, you will keep my commandments" (John 14:15).

My appeal is that you look to Jesus for eternal life. Worship him as your Lord and God. Call on Him while He is near. Now is the day of salvation! To learn more, find the Gospel of John in the Bible. Read one chapter at a time. At the end of each chapter, ask yourself two questions: Based on this chapter, who is Jesus? What does He want from me? There are 21 chapters in John's Gospel. Will you accept a 21-Day Challenge and read a chapter a day?

Free Resources at NTRF.org

Articles: Various Church-Life Topics

Audio Series: Bi-Vocational Shepherding Help

Bible Studies: Bible Book Discussion/Study
Guides for Teachers

Discussion Guide: The Practice of the Early Church

Pamphlet: The Lord's Supper: An Actual Meal

Video Series: Ancient Church Strategies for Effective
Ministry

Workshop: How to Lead a Bible Discussion